Praise for

"While I expected to laugh my way through Carolanne Miljavac's latest offering, I didn't anticipate the wealth of hard-earned insight and biblical wisdom coming from one of my favorite funny young women, all delivered without a filter in sight to better serve those living and learning with her. Well done, friend. Honored to co-labor with you in this glorious gospel of Jesus Christ."

–Shellie Rushing Tomlinson, author of
Finding Deep and Wide

"I read Carolanne's book in the midst of a mental breakdown. I had been trying to control everything around me and seemed to have lost myself in the process. Not only did I find myself laughing and relating to Carolanne's hilarious stories (like hobbling around with dog and husband pee on her feet), but her ability to laugh through the chaos and learn from each situation taught me that it's okay to trust in something bigger than me and enjoy the ride, even when I'm not sure where it's headed. This book came at the perfect time."

–Tiffany Jenkins of "Juggling the Jenkins,"
author of *High Achiever*, influencer, podcast
host, and advocate for life after addiction

"The Bible says a joyful heart and laughter are good medicine, and *She Laughs* is definitely ibuprofen for the soul. It's inspirational, biblically sound, and downright funny. I know it will bless readers in whatever season they find themselves."

–Susannah Lewis of Whoa Susannah,
author of *Can't Make This Stuff Up*

"I laughed out loud so many times. Her writing feels like I'm sitting at a coffee shop with my best friend feeling so comfortable and understood."

–Adley Stump, The Adley Show

She Laughs

CHOOSING FAITH OVER FEAR

Carolanne Miljavac

SHILOH RUN PRESS
An Imprint of Barbour Publishing, Inc.

Cover Design: Greg Jackson, Thinkpen Design

Published by Shiloh Run Press, an imprint of Barbour Publishing, Inc., 1810 Barbour
Drive, Uhrichsville, Ohio 44683, www.shilohrunpress.com

Our mission is to inspire the world with the life-changing message of the Bible.

Member of the
Evangelical Christian
Publishers Association

Printed in the United States of America.

IN LOVING MEMORY OF
ANSLEY ABIGAIL SMITH

CONTENTS

INTRODUCTION

She is clothed with strength and dignity,
and she laughs without fear of the future.
PROVERBS 31:25

We live in a culture overwhelmed with knowledge. Anything we wanna know, all we gotta do is ask Siri or Alexa. . .or if you're an eighties baby like me, you might still manually google it with your fingertips. Wanna know a play-by-play of your high school crush? I don't, but I'm just sayin' if *you* do, it's probably a quick glance at MyFace, InstaChat, SnapTok, or a Tweeter away. Hey, what's this rash on my kid's arm? Oh, okay, it could be carpet burn, could be a flesh-eating virus. Thanks, internets, I feel much better. We know almost everyone's each and every thought, opinion, annoyance, political stance, food preference, bathroom schedule, parenting dos and you-better-nots, financial status, et cetera, et cetera. (Sidenote: How in the world with all of this information does my husband still not know what I want from Subway?)

With all of this info overload, does anyone else find

themselves running in circles confused, conflicted, overwhelmed, doubtful, worried, anxious, and worst of all, *afraid*? But scripture says, "She laughs." This Proverbs woman we all aspire to be laughs fearlessly. I want what she has. I want to have peace. How can I get a little closer to making *she. . .*me? In certain seasons of life, you may feel like you've lost her. But I promise she is always there. I'll tell you what I've learned about her through my own journey of hilarious stories. I pray it will help you laugh again. A woman who has joy has peace in her heart. As long as you have the ability to laugh, there's hope for joy in your future.

Chapter 1

She Is Restored

I trust in you, my God! Do not let me be disgraced,
or let my enemies rejoice in my defeat.
PSALM 25:2

I woke up late as usual to the sound of my mama threat-ening my life if I stayed in bed one minute longer: *"Git up and git ready before I drag you out of bed by your ankle bone!"* I had already managed by 7:30 a.m. to shat-ter any hopes my mom had that day of keeping her joy, living in peace, and not yelling. (Don't worry, I have three little girls now, so I'm "payin' for my raisin,'" as we say in the South.) Turns out this was one of those days when none of my three pairs of underwears were clean, so I just had to go commando. Meh, no biggie. Not something I stressed about. So I slipped on my loose-fitting, tie-string, popular-from-The-Gap pants my friend gave me that could easily slip down and accidentally show my crack. . . because what's the worst that could happen?

Backstory: It's homecoming week, so at the end of every day, the whole high school gathers in the gym for a pep rally. The cheerleaders shake their rear ends in the football players' faces, the football players sit back elbowing each other like, "Dude. Cheerleaders. Butts. Britney Spears. Yes, dude." And there was always a crazy-funny game where two people from each grade were called out to the middle of the gym to compete for their class. As I sat in sixth period getting ready to head to the pep rally, I got some sixth sense that my period was about to make an unexpected appearance. Just so y'all know, I was the class clown but not popular. I wasn't secure in myself. I didn't have any good friends in that sixth-period class, so I tried to just take care of things myself instead of asking for help. I rushed to the bathroom and, sure 'nuff, it was a code red. Good ol' Aunt Flo decided to drop in early to ruin my whole life. Obviously, like any stressed-out genius fourteen-year-old girl would, I decided to just roll up a pound of toilet paper and put it in my pants to hold me over until I could get to a tampon or a pad. Except on this one day, I didn't have any underwear on, and I was wearing loose-fitting pants. Face palm. I was all alone in the gym bathroom stall sweating, trying to breathe, telling myself not to panic. *You got this, Carolanne. You can just walk with your legs as close together as possible and sit still until the pep rally is over. Yeah, good plan, you can do this.* So I walked nonchalantly out of the bathroom like I just had a colonoscopy, cool as a cucumber, nothing to see here, and took a seat on the bleachers closest to the door. They started to call out the names for the pep rally game. One boy and one girl from each grade. It dawned on me in that moment that there was actually a small chance I could be the name called out. But that had never ever happened before. So I just started thinking over and over, *Don't say me. Don't say me. Don't say me.* It turns out I have an ability to will things to happen with my thoughts, because I'll be derned if of all the days this could have happened, they didn't call out, "Representing the freshmen girls, Carol Upton!" The entire freshman class looked over at me, clapping, cheering, laughing, and pushing me out there. My entire body got hot as I Gumby-walked out into the middle of the gym floor with my guy partner, hoping and praying the game wouldn't involve running. My thighs squeezed so tight a crowbar couldn't break 'em open. I looked around smiling like, *Yeah, we got this, we're gonna win, and I don't have period paper holding on for dear life in my pants, I swear.* They announced that we were going to have a dance-off. A dance-off, y'all. Blindfolded. With your partner. (Guess embarrassing dancing has always been a part of my story, considering most of you know it, I'll moon y'all again tomorrow." Hardy-har. All the while my thoughts raced frantically: *My naked butt. My buck-naked butt. They all saw it. Wonder if they thought it was a good butt or. . .wait, what? No, I gotta go. I gotta get outta here.* You ever have a code red situation that left you in need of restoration? Maybe it wasn't quite on this level of nightmare embarrassment, but I'm sure you've had plenty of experiences that left you feeling like hiding under a rock for a while. If there's one way to recover from complete humiliation, it's an ability to laugh about it.

That wasn't the first time I embarrassed myself in a gym full of classmates.

The gym is packed at Maddox Middle School for our first basketball game of the season, and *I. Am. Pumped.* It only took me until eighth grade to finally muster up the courage to take my ridiculous b-ball skills from my granny's driveway to an actual court. I just wasn't sure the team would be prepared for all this talent. I mean, ask my mama, I sink it nothing but net from halfway across PawPaw's yard forty percent of the time—every single time. Apparently in a real game, there are rules, plays, and other things than just shooting—like dribbling and stuff. Those things didn't come as easily to me, so for our first game, I started off on the bench. Totally fine. No worries at all. It wasn't like I wanted to waltz in with all this natural talent and take a starting position from one of the girls who had been playing all her life. So I sat on the edge of the bench, heart pounding, waiting for Coach to give me a chance to show him what I could do. Finally, he turns to me and says, "Carol! Sub in for Sam." *Oh, okay, this is it, it's happening!* I immediately shot off the bench, sprinted straight out onto the court, and stopped the game midplay, announcing to Sam that she's out, I'm in. My time to shine. Take a seat. Party's here. Everyone, including the ref, just stood there staring at me with a look of confusion mixed with a stifled chuckle. *Um, what is happening? What did I do?* Something embarrassing, I could feel it. I turned to look at my coach, and he was motioning for me to come back while grinning ear to ear. Nobody ever told me you had to wait on the side for the ref to check you in when it's time. As I took my jog of shame back to the check-in spot, I could feel every person in the gym looking and laughing at my failed attempt at playing in my first-ever basketball game.

Or how about the other time I rammed my

forehead into a metal flagpole right in front of my crush? Yeah. In junior college. I was trying to be all flirty and cute while walking into the school building by turning around to look at him and smiling with my long, flowing hair fluttering in the wind. My slow-mo love gaze was working too, until I turned around only to plow my face right into the flagpole so hard that my head bounced back and the pole sounded off a loud *diiiiing*. Pretty sure he was grinning back at me because he knew I was about to walk into that pole. Jerk. I had to sit through class holding an ice pack on the red lump growing out of my forehead. I actually hurt myself trying to flirt. You'd think I would have learned not to look at this guy after almost running my car into the ditch in front of the baseball players' apartments on my way to class when he walked out shirtless. I didn't mean to turn the whole wheel with the turning of my head. These days kids endanger others while texting and driving; back in my day, we got distracted by real-life muscles.

Humiliation isn't always a funny story. It's not just a red face when you walk into a flagpole. It's also how you feel when you've been overlooked, pushed aside, or outright rejected. Has there been a time in your life when you weren't chosen, and it chipped away at your value?

that I truly felt I'd never overcome it.

From fourth grade to seventh grade, I decided it would be easier to just keep to myself and get through each day than to risk being rejected in any way. Nothing felt more humiliating to me than rejection. I scared myself straight into seclusion. It wasn't risky; it was easy. And although it was lonely, it was my choice. I would watch the other kids in my class seem to be able to just naturally express themselves. I found that so frustrating. I couldn't speak without first imagining all the many ways people might react to me. Would they agree, laugh, respond, or—the worst thing possible—ignore me? The idea of saying something among my peers and being completely ignored terrified me, because that would mean I wasn't worthy enough to even be acknowledged. That I might as well not even exist. So as I sat quietly in the corner of math class, so in my own head that I couldn't even look at anyone, I wondered, *Why am I like this?*

Once a stronghold of insecurity gets into your head, it is really tough to overcome. You just feel like you can't help it. Your thoughts and feelings seem out of control. And that was it. Control. I was trying so hard to be in control by choosing to hide. But I realized that in hiding, I wasn't in control at all. My fears were. Hypothetical reactions that could maybe possibly happen were putting me in a corner. It was only in the middle of one embarrassing moment after another that I realized nothing was in my control. So what was the point? I wasn't happy overthinking all alone. I wouldn't be happy if people didn't like me either, but at least I would have given myself a chance. If I opened my mouth and found myself in a "funny or flight" situation, I was gonna choose to laugh. Because laughter is contagious, and surely someone at some point would join me. That's how choosing to see the humor restores us. It helps us be brave enough to set aside worries and show up, insecurities and all.

What is it about rejection that you are afraid of? Is it a pride thing? Is it a people thing? Is it a skill set thing? Is it an idea that you just know is good, but *they* might not validate it? Is it a job you want so bad because you just know you were made for it, but *they* might not see your potential?

Who is this "they" who might reject you and ruin your whole purpose of existence? If *they* aren't God. . . Oh, this is about to get good. If *they* are not Him, then *they* do not matter. He does not reject you. He does not turn away from you. He knows your value.

> And having chosen them, he called them to
> come to him. And having called them, he gave
> them right standing with himself. And having
> given them right standing, he gave them his
> glory. What shall we say about such wonderful
> things as these? If God is for us, who can ever
> be against us? (Romans 8:30–31)

This scripture confirms that God gave you a destiny before you were even born. Before anyone heard the flutter of your heart, you were already called. Wow. How does that feel? To know that your worth has already been written, your purpose justified. Would you still be scared if you believed that rejection of the world only brings you closer to the glory of God's plan for your life? Who could possibly keep you in a corner, when He who knit you in your mother's womb says you have a purpose? Knowing that scripture and walking in that scripture are two very different things. You have to believe it. Your absent dad, peers, coworkers, ex-boyfriends, and worst enemies do not determine your value. Who can reject you when you've been accepted into the University of Jesus through mercy and grace? They can turn you down, sure. They can tell you no. They can walk away, break promises, shut doors, and hurt your feelings. But He will heal your heart and show you a better way—away from *they*. The Holy Spirit will overwhelm every rejection of your flesh. The door they closed just allowed you to focus on the one God was about to open. The no they just said got you closer to a better yes. Those who walked away weren't supposed to be there in the first place. Rejection simply sets you off in a different direction. Sometimes it takes a detour to get where you're going with a fresh perspective, so when you arrive, you're ready to serve in a way you weren't previously prepared for. You can laugh when they close a door, because every bit of value they denied will be restored. Keep your faith and one day you'll look back and laugh at how glad you are that the job, relationship, or opportunity you thought you wanted didn't pan out. What does that look like in your life right now? Is there something that didn't work out in your past that set up the path to a much better door in your future?

Do you know that even when things are not okay today, there will come a time when you will be okay again?

You will be okay.

You are okay.

And we know that God causes everything to work together for the good of those who love God and are called according to his purpose for them. (Romans 8:28)

That verse doesn't say "we *think*" or "we *hope*"—it says we *know*. I want you to think of the hardest thing you have ever been through in your past. Do you remember a situation that felt truly hopeless? I can't tell you how many times I've thought to myself, *I don't know how we are going to make it through this*, or *What are we going to do?* Sitting up late at night worrying my sanity away because I didn't think praying would matter.

As a girl, I could glimpse a future for myself, but I also feared failure. I feared rejection.

I'm not a fan of disappointing people. I mean, the whole reason I fell in love with comedy as a child was because it helped me feel accepted. I used to watch Carol Burnett, Gilda Radner, and Lucille Ball with such admiration. The way they were able to let loose, be silly, and put themselves out there while giving people joy was so appealing to me. When I was laughing at them, I wasn't worried about struggling with insecurity at school the next day. And any pain I harbored momentarily faded away. They gave me peace just being goofy. I loved them for that. I had such a strong desire to do what they were doing. One, because I felt validated every time my mom or siblings laughed at me. Two, because I wanted to help others feel the peace that laughter brings, the way I did. I would lie on my granny's trampoline all day, staring at the clouds and daydreaming about breaking away from my little country town and making it big goofing off on *SNL*. That dream felt bigger than the sky. But when I actually imagined the risks it would take to make it happen, the fear of falling overcame the exhilaration of the calling. I was too afraid I'd fall short if I pursued being a comedian. If I tell that joke, make that face, or act out that story with the downright goofiness that makes up a huge part of my identity, and I get crickets, then I've been deeply rejected. So I settled for being class clown, doing skits for the team in the dugout, and being the comedic relief when situations got tense with family or friends. The problem was that I wasn't seeking the Lord within my passion. I was seeking approval. That need to be accepted by the world kept me locked in a cage, afraid of shame.

When I let God in and gave up all of myself to His will, that feeling of fear faded to faith in who He created me to be. Notice I said that it faded, not that it disappeared. Stepping into your calling is the scariest feeling. Making the choice to believe in yourself comes with the challenge of recovering from as much failure as it takes to develop your gifts. I've never felt more vulnerable than when standing on a stage under lights with a mic, telling jokes or lifting others up. Backstage I try telling myself to calm down, to not let the nerves overwhelm my ability, to take deep breaths and slow down my heartbeat. It doesn't work. But I've learned it's not a crippling fear I'm feeling. It's an excited fear. With the first step onto the stage, I come through the anxiety and feel at home. And I am so in awe that God loves us so much, He gives us opportunities to experience purpose.

Fear feels pretty hopeless, but God's voice causes fear to melt as He restores us with our purpose.

Gosh, I've felt so hopeless at different times in my life. I had less than $50 to my name when I found out I was pregnant with my first daughter. My boyfriend (now husband) wasn't making much playing shows on the weekend while recording an album with his band. Fun fact, record deals don't mean you get paid. I worried relentlessly while searching for a job. Found one in outside sales, worked my butt off, and saved up enough cash to have an apartment ready for a baby.

Then my anxiety moved on to how we'd ever afford a crib. I was so tired, so pregnant, and so depleted. Then my coworkers threw me a baby shower, and everyone in the office pitched in to get us a crib *and* a dresser, decorations, blankets, and diapers. In that moment I laughed hysterically as the tears poured, and in an instant, all hope was restored.

At the most stressful times in my life, somehow there was always the exact right person or people around me to help me through. Have you ever felt really scared about a situation, and out of nowhere a solution appeared? Or you happened to read the exact thing you needed? Or a text arrived with an encouraging word from a friend? Or you realized later that what you couldn't see was that you are always going to have what you *need*. One way or another, there's nothing you've been through that you didn't get through.

The woman who can throw her head back and laugh knows there's a plan for her. She knows there will be good times and bad. She doesn't fear the bad, because she is rooted in the truth that even through the worst, there's so much more good. Those called according to God's purpose will always be shown a way to make something of their pain. So today, lay down your worry and lean on what you *know*. God is good. His plans for you are good. Troubles will come and go, but one thing consistently stays true. He loves you.

Y'all ever had a massage? I hate 'em. Great for your body. Loosen up some muscles, flush out some toxins, release some endorphins. Great for *restoration*. Torture getting through it. Mentally, physically, emotionally, all of it. Just horrible. I'm not a manicure-pedicure-spa-experience type of gal. But it was my and my husband's first vacation *ever*. We never had a honeymoon or anything, so I really wanted to go all out and try new things while we were in Mexico. He loves massages, so against my better judgment, I scheduled us for a nice relaxing appointment to have a stranger rub us down while stark naked under a sheet in the same room together. I thought I could be a grown adult woman and unwind during it. I was wrong. First of all, we were in Mexico. So my Southern butt embarrassingly can't understand most of what anyone is saying, and I find it mortifying. I will apologetically say, "I'm sorry, I didn't hear you," no more than two times before I panic and just say, "Okay, thank you." We walked into the massage room, him in a robe, me still fully clothed with no idea why I didn't get a robe and too afraid to ask because I probably wouldn't understand the answer. We listened intently as she explained to us what to do before they came back, and the only word I caught was *naked*. She said okay and looked at us, we said okay as if we had a clue what to do, and she left. As the door shut, my husband and I turned and looked at each other wide-eyed and I said, "We just get naked? Like underwear too? Is that what she said? Do we lie on our stomach? I'm freaking out." To which he grinned and shrugged his shoulders. Y'all, I've never felt so awkward in my life. I know what you're thinking. He's your husband; you have three kids. None of that matters, okay? I'm modest, and these things make me want to die. We began to disrobe, and not in a sexy way. Rushing to strip off my clothes in a large open room with no idea how much time I have until a stranger walks back in is not my idea of romantic. I slung my clothes in a corner, slowed down enough to tuck my undies in my pants like ladies do, and dove under the sheet facedown. When the ladies came back, I was ready to be done. Turns out this was an all-out sixty-minute, full-body massage. Head and shoulders to shins and toes. *Kill me now.* My husband snoring loudly beside me as I tried to hide my self-tanned disaster of a thumb during the hand massage. She must've asked if I was okay at least six times while trying to pry my Cheeto-orange thumb out of my palm. I walked out of that massage riddled with tension, my husband loose as a goose. Now it is confirmed for me that I do not, in fact, ever in any circumstance enjoy a massage. Restoration doesn't always feel good. When you aren't ready to let go of fear, insecurity, or rejection, you carry the tension in your spirit. But there's a gift to help you relax while God tries to work all the strongholds out of you. Laughter. Humor is like the oil that helps Him work out the kinks so the aches of the process aren't quite so deep. The massage message here is that you've been given laughter as a buffer through the pain of restoration. There's no heart too hardened for laughter to restore.

She laughs without fear of what the future holds, because with faith her worth is always restored.

Chapter 2

She Plays

"I tell you the truth, unless you turn from your
sins and become like little children, you will
never get into the Kingdom of Heaven."
MATTHEW 18:3

"Rock, paper, scissors, shoot. Cheater."

"Rock, paper, scissors. . .you cheat! I can see you
with my eyeballs changing what you're gonna do at the
last second. You can't change to scissors when you see
my hand going for paper!"

I guess cheating is the only way my kids can win
games against me, since I refuse to let them win. Atti-
tudes in response to failure are a much more important
lesson to learn. Who better to teach them than the girl
who once threw, or "accidentally aggressively knocked
over," a deck of cards while playing the memory game
with her granny? But I mean, how frustrating to lose the
memory game to your *granny*. She always laughed when
I said that to her. We had a connection like that. We
could poke at each other with quick wit and sarcasm.
Some of the best connections in life are with people
you click with so well that you can ruffle each other's

feathers and just cackle over it. We are a game-playing family. A family that plays together gets mad at each other, but then laughs together.

My granny Wanda was a gamer back when gaming meant "adults only" playing dominoes, spades, and poker for money at the kitchen table. I wanted to play so bad I couldn't stand it. I'd circle the table looking at everyone's cards as a potential threat tactic. So, deep down they knew if they didn't let me play, I might "accidentally" slip up like, "Whoopsie, I didn't know any better," and ruin their game. At the same time, I would ask if I could play at least three times every eight minutes. All kids know it takes one hundred nos to get to a yes. . .or to get locked in a room. They will risk lockdown for the yes every single time.

During the day, my granny Wanda and I would sit with a deck of cards and play Memory, Go Fish, and War. We'd play dominoes, do crossword puzzles, and watch the Whammy game show. We'd sit in the living room and both pick who we wanted to win, and then when our person hit their button and the light bee-boop-bee-booped around the points board, we'd chant, "No whammies, no whammies, noooo whammies." But *Wheel of Fortune* was our favorite game show, and we took it pretty seriously. "One does not simply say two words of the puzzle and then take credit for solving half of it." If you do that, you can't watch with us.

Long after Granny had passed and I was in junior college, I met a best friend / roommate / soul sister on my softball team who shared my love and respect for the rules of *Wheel of Fortune*. It was our favorite thing to do every night after practice. We'd race back to our apartment, whip up some Tuna Helper, take our place in our separate recliners, and just look at each other all giddy while our teammates went to a different room to be around normal people. As the show began, we'd put on our game face with our hand on our chair's recliner handle and count down, "Three, two, one. . ." Out shot our footrests at the same time we chanted, "Wheel. Of. Fortune!!!" The next thirty minutes went like this. . .

"Pepper, peppermint stick shift!" "Nah-uh, we got that at the same time." "Shhhhhhhiitake mushroom!!! That's it. Oh my gosh. That's it! I just solved it and there weren't even any letters up. I am the queen of the Wheel." "It was 'shiitake mushroomssssss.' With an *s*. I win." "That doesn't even matter, Brittanyyyyyy." If this isn't you and your best friend, are you even friends?

But above all games ever created, the one that

forever holds a special place in my family's heart is Aggravation. Does your family have something that all of you instantly connect to? It just immediately reminds you of each other or is sort of this tangible symbol of your clan. Each of us has a specific character that comes out when playing this board game.

1. I'm the fit-pitcher. I am aware of this. I know this. I'm working on it. I always begin the game determined to play only for fun. But before I know it, my brother-in-law, JR, is chanting, "Shake 'n' bake," while knocking me out the fourth time in a row and I find myself huffing, "Pick on someone else. Heck, I ain't gonna win—go knock out Mama!" Then my lovely family begins to poke me, saying, "Don't get mad," which really makes me mad, so I yell, "I'm not mad. Y'all 're about to *make* me mad!" Then I pitch a fit.

2. My mama is the prophet. She speaks over herself the entire game, and it drives me nuts. "All right, I need a five. Give me a five. Five, five, five." Then I'll be derned if she doesn't roll a five, do a little dance, and then giggle at the rest of us. "I told y'all you just gotta talk to your dice." Me beside her with my stank face trying so hard to remember to just have fun.

3. My sister straight whines the whole time. "Y'allll,

I'm not even out of base yet. JR, uh, donnnn't. I just got out."

4. My brother-in-law plays for no other reason than to knock everyone out as much as he can. He is just there to mess stuff up while quoting *Talladega Nights*.

5. My stepdad is the slowpoke. We can see the algorithms floating above his head as he contemplates which move will be most beneficial for him four plays from that one. If we don't collectively say, "Go!" I'm not sure the game would ever end. And since he's a massive Auburn fan, we make sure to say "Roll Tide" every time we take him down.

6. My niece, Lacy, says nothing. She is the invisible winner who slides under everyone else's radar while we are busy pitching fits, chanting, whining, imitating Ricky Bobby, and doing algebra.

It's the funnest thing we do together, and we love every single second of it.

That old, folded-up cardboard and those marbles and dice have brought us many laughs despite hard times. When financial struggles tried to steal our light, we just played in the dark.

A family of four sat on the floor, tears running down their cheeks. Laughing hysterically as the light of the flickering candles bounced off the water falling from their faces to their feet. I know what you must think. But this isn't a picture of a family without peace. No. This is a family capable of laughter regardless of their grief. My mom may have worked two or three jobs at a time, but it didn't keep us out of poverty. We spent many nights making the most of our life without lights. Almost every time Alabama Power came rolling through, I knew exactly what they were about to do. So began the scramble to get out all the candles before the sun went down. Truly, it really isn't that bad having the power turned off. The worst part was not knowing what was in the fridge and not being able to open the door because, "Yer lettin' the cold air out!" But when the convenient things that filled up our attention were removed, we had some of the best nights together. We'd open the windows, make some sandwiches, sit on the floor, and cackle over a candlelit card game. Instead of worrying, fussing, and whining the night away, we'd play.

For our family, an appreciation for play is rooted in the ability it gives us to be present. To remember what matters most—time with each other, memories, and laughter. Something so simple as a game can bring you joy when you need it the most. Especially in the middle of loss.

We will never forget something that happened at my PaPa Bob's funeral. Our family is pretty small. My mom, two aunts, and a few cousins basically make up the whole family. We gathered, grew up, and spent countless hours under Granny Peggy and PaPa Bob's roof. We are a pretty gritty group, but when I walked into the funeral home and saw his name next to the door, the sorrow rose up through my chest, and I couldn't control the outburst of tears that followed. We all had our moments throughout that visitation. But as the end of the day neared and more people were catching up and talking, it felt like just another family gathering that my papa was hosting. We sat in the pews telling hilarious stories that happened at PaPa and Granny's house.

Stories about the old trampoline death trap out back with missing springs that we'd spray with the hose pipe and try to knock each other off with basketballs and anything else we could throw. No safety nets or helicopter moms for us. Just Granny inside the locked house watching *Murder, She Wrote* and smoking her Virginia Slims.

Then there was the time I begged and begged my mama to let me say just one curse word. My papa sat in his old blue recliner puffing on a Black & Mild, just shaking his head and grinning as I whined my way to three minutes of foul-mouthed freedom. But *only* for one word. *Dayum.* That's the Southern pronunciation. Y'all, I sprinted out the screen door and ran circles around my papa's house using that bad word as much as humanly possible. I chanted a lil hillbilly ditty that went like this (earmuffs, kids): "Dayumdad**d**d**, look at that d*** grass, over there's some d*** dog poop, dang that d*** sky's blue, there's my d*** neighbor, d*** David is his name." It was one of the best d*** days of my life.

We cackled talking about the scary Halloween home video commercial we made when we were kids on my grandparents' porch. PaPa set the spooky scenery in his yard each year by piling all the leaves into pumpkin, ghost, and black cat trash bags. My aunt wrapped the pillars on the porch with stretchy fake spiderwebs, so the background was all set. Our commercial began with a young girl (me) scraping her face off on her grand-parents' driveway during an intense basketball scram-ble with her little brother. The action started with me screaming bloody murder, lying facedown on the ce-ment. My big sis flipped me over, and to everyone's horror, half of my face was gone! The camera dropped

on our family reunion Facebook page. "You can tell Patsy an' 'em they better not be there—they ain't even our kin." It's like an episode of *Jerry Springer* on there.

I guess a sense of humor during tough times isn't always understood by everyone. But it's something my family really holds dear. When you come from nothing, lose loved ones often, and experience trauma, an ability to put all those emotions aside and play keeps your spirit from the darkness that threatens to steal your joy away. You ever hear the sounds of a playground? Aside from the germaphobe mom freaking out as little Billy chews a piece of gum he found under a slide, it's full of gleeful giggles, squeals, and cackles of laughter. Laughter and play go together like ball pits and hand sanitizer. Like distressed wood and HGTV. Like nice hands and QVC. Like grown men and pee on the toilet seat. Know what I'm sayin'? Can't have one without the other, and where there's laughter there's happy. So when you have a chance to play, it's important to get into the game.

The first week my niece spent at Saint Jude was really traumatic for her. She had several surgeries and a tracheotomy and almost died. When I visited, she couldn't speak and barely acknowledged anyone because she was so sad and scared. I went to the play area and grabbed the game Connect Four. I pulled up a chair next to her hospital bed, and she actually rolled over to play. Five straight games that child won. It only took me four games of sorely losing to get her to crack the tiniest of smirks. That moment mattered. She had a long, hard journey ahead of her, and being able to play in the smallest way let her know it was okay to smile again.

That hospital is full of children who are sad, sick, and dying. Why do you think it's so important for them to continue to play? Even in isolation, Ansley had markers to decorate her window and automatic sliding door. Child-life specialists visit to sing songs, play music, and do all they can to help these children continue to laugh. The halls are decorated with colorful splashes and light-hearted murals. Toddlers attached to medicine bags ride in little red wagons to the playroom full of books and toys. Why?

Children nurture their fun-loving spirits with toys, imagination, and games. If they can't play, they'll just think about how sick they are all day. Their joy is at stake. Stress, worry, and negative brain activity can actually harm the immune system and make a person physically feel worse. When children play, they aren't thinking about cancer, death, what they miss, or how bad they want to go home. They are just enjoying the moment.

The day we buried Ansley, we all went to my sister's house afterward. We sat around her kitchen table tossing dice, moving marbles, wiping away the occasional runaway tear, and laughing together. Aggravation was the momentary distraction from our devastation. It helped us physically get through the hours following her funeral. That night all of us went bowling. Our whole family. I know a lot of people might think that's kind of weird, but her loss was the harshest pain any of us had ever felt. We needed to be together. We needed to lean on each other. Being out and in public playing a game of bowling helped us have faith that although hollow days of overwhelming sadness were ahead, we'd be okay again. Because we got through those first few days, we could get through each one to follow. Especially my sister's family. I believe the presence of laughter was our saving grace.

When was the last time you played? Has it been a while since you put the adult away and got in touch with your childish side? I don't know what kind of joy-suckers you've been dealing with, but maybe it's time for a break from the seriousness of this adult life.

As a mom of three, I've had so many weeks when I've sat down and felt like a crappy parent because I was too distracted, overwhelmed, or stressed to play with my kids. Especially when it's those pesky little glittery, peeing, spitting LOL Dolls that my girls are obsessed with opening. They want me to produce an entertaining pretend play scenario out of thin air. As if that's not enough, I have to do it in a *whiny voice.* Just for perspective, the only time I played with Barbies when I was little was when I hid all their clothes to tick off my sister. I don't like playing with dolls; I like playing games. Uno I'm in, but getting "Vacay Babay" up and ready for her first day of school is a no. I have the hardest time thinking of things to say, so I just say, "Yeah. Okay. Um, so I think it's time for Glitter baby's nap." Then I tell them that while she's napping, I'm gonna go use the bathroom and never come back until one of them notices. "Oh. Sorry, I thought she was still napping." Thanks a lot by the way to the famous YouTube parents for setting such unrealistic playtime standards for the rest of us big dull duds. Sorry, girls, I love you, but we are not doing the spend-the-night-in-a-tree challenge. That perfect patty family only did it because they make tons of money from all the kids watching it wishing *their* family was this cool. Parenting is tough, I tell ya. Listen here, we do the best we can. I don't do dolls well, but I do badminton, tag, card games, and my favorite game of all, Quiet as a Mouse, Still as a Rock. And that's okay.

If you're married or dating, when was the last time you played with your significant other? Game night, comedy show, mini golf, whatever the two of you have fun doing helps take your thoughts away from the ways you drive each other nuts. Seriously though, laughing together is so important. Sometimes it's the only method of mending a season of mistakes. If I am determined to be mad at my husband, but then this comic on TV tells a joke about his wife trying to slam the slow-close toilet lid in a fit of anger and we both lose it because I did that, it's hard for me to stay mad. In that moment when we are both laughing together at the same thing, whether I like it or not, we are connected. It's hard to hang on to anger when you're laughing together. To all the single ladies, when is the last time you played with your friends? Joining a bunko group can be tough. You gotta wait for an opening and then try out, then wait for your acceptance letter. But maybe just a trivia night, some snacks, a good movie, and some Jenga? Or my all-time favorite, Dave & Buster's!

Who doesn't want to play a giant digital game of Connect Four?! Even the workplace needs to take a break to play together. That's why so many businesses have team nights to foster play. It helps restore a joyful, creative, motivated atmosphere.

I have to tell y'all something. It's an actual fantasy of mine to live in a small country town that hosts outdoor Bingo nights in the summer. I wanna get a group of Bingo friends together so bad. I just think it would be so much fun. I'd be front row with five different cards and a specialized bingo marker just like the one my granny Wanda had. But I can't seem to find many other women my age who want to join me. Guess they aren't ready to admit we have reached the HGTV, QVC, Food Network, and Bingo Nights season of life.

I do have a group of gal pals I play volleyball with each summer. Our team name is Mom's Night Out, and it truly is the one night of the week we get to get out, have some fun, and catch up. It's not about winning—although, if you ask my teammates, I don't smile as much when we get our butts kicked. They always say I have the worst look on my face, but it's really just the sand in my eyes. . .as well as the horrible score. I can't help my expressive face. It's a gift and a curse. Great for telling stories, horrible for hiding irritation.

Not everyone plays or enjoys sports, but I will forever hold a special place in my heart for every sport I played growing up. Especially softball. My mom signed me up when I was ten, and I still remember the day she looked in the rearview mirror at me in the backseat and asked if I wanted to play. I had never been so excited about anything in my life. The very first practice I got my nose busted. It was awesome. On the field I could escape. It didn't matter that I was poor, I didn't have to fit in, and I had a coach to look up to. Someone to believe in me, teach me, encourage me, and give me direction. I could get dirty, run fast, throw hard, and release all the troubles, insecurities, and secrets haunting my thoughts. That's what any kind of playing has always been for me—an escape. Playing sets me free.

Matthew 18:3 says to become like children. Children can play and play and play all day long. Why do you think that is? I think it's because they can. They naturally tend to take action toward the things they know they enjoy. Like running through parking lots before you've put their leash on. Okay, it's not a leash; it's a monkey backpack lifesaving device, and there's no telling how many times that tail wrapped around my wrist has saved my toddler from a tailgate. Children know what brings them joy, and they seek it out. Like chewing their food into liquid before spitting it into the cupholder of their car seat.

Kids love to laugh. And what better segue to laughter than play? Children are open to learning. For example, Mommy will not let you hide with me during hide-and-seek. You go find your own spot; you're giving mine away.

If we were more childlike in our faith, we'd be more willing to lean on the truth. We wouldn't let so many things fog up our connection with the Lord. We'd follow Him relentlessly. Even if He's just trying to use the bathroom or take a shower. We'd keep Him near at all times. Sit on His feet when He walks, sleep on His face, freak out if we found ourselves too far away—like from the couch to the kitchen. When we wanted to be held, we'd simply lift up our arms and ask.

I was at a conference once when a friend who was new in her faith told me she felt such an urge during worship to let go of her hesitations and lift up her hands in praise. But she just couldn't do it, for fear. Fear of the people around her and what they'd think. Fear of being vulnerable. Fear of letting those walls come down so she could freely and openly let the Lord fill her up and love on her. I asked her what it was she wanted to feel from God more than anything in the world. She said love. She wanted to feel loved. She wanted to be embraced like in a great big hug. So I asked her what children do when they walk up to their parents and want a hug or to be lifted up. She grinned and answered, "They lift up their hands."

Yes. They lift up their hands. Be more childlike in your faith. Do not be ashamed. When your soul is thirsty for love, needing to be embraced, lift your hands up to the Lord and sing His praise. Cut off the chains keeping your arms stuck in place. Sometimes that is all it takes. If you are feeling a stirring as you read this, I bet you could use some good vulnerable praise. He wants to fill you up and give you peace, but you gotta allow Him to. Toddlers know their mommy won't turn them away. They know without a doubt they are loved. They know that no matter how full Mama's hands are, she is gonna pick that baby up. Now I might have almost dropped mine a time or two, but there's only so much we can do. Nothing an LOL Band-Aid won't make better. I always said God gives us childbearing hips so we can balance the baby on one and the world on the other. But sometimes we just need to put the world away, take a break, and play.

We are children of God. We are loved. Our Father in heaven will always lift us up. Work, bills, to-do lists, phone calls, and everything else can wait. If we can get back to the basics of what really, really matters to us, we will be able to soak in moments that last forever.

When serious stress begins to steal away her joy, *she laughs* while *she plays.*

Chapter 3

─888─

SHE SPEAKS

When she speaks, her words are wise,
and she gives instructions with kindness.
PROVERBS 31:26

It was pouring down rain one morning on the way to drop off my kids at school. I was on a side road waiting for traffic to give me an opening to turn left. I looked left, then right, then left again, then right again because I'm a paranoid driver, and then began to pull out and turn. All of a sudden, out of nowhere, in the middle of the road is a whole entire human being standing in front of my car. I slammed on my brakes and turned the wheel to the right, giving her just a tiny little tap on the back of her butt. I'd call it a nudge, really. Just enough to let her know it's not a good idea to go for a jaywalk in the pouring rain. Let's just say I've seen harder flops in the NBA than the amount of bounce she did off my bumper. I'm polite, so even though I knew she was okay, I rolled down my window to make sure she was, in fact, alive and well. She seemed fine. Her voice box definitely wasn't broken, because I clearly heard every syllable of the vulgarity she shouted at me. I was thinking, *Whoa*

whoa whoa, I've got kids in the car. Watch the language, and a "thank you for not killing me" would be nice. But what I said was, "I'm so sorry, I didn't see you! I didn't see you in the rain! You're okay? Okay. Get home safe!" My girls in the back encouraged me, saying, "You're okay, Mom. It's okay. You're okay." Listen, I reminded that girl how precious life is. Thanks to me, I bet she thinks of every moment as a gift. But just in case she was super angry and out for revenge, I did the right thing and called the police on myself. I told them I tapped a pedestrian just a little bit on the back of her butt, so if anyone called to say they got hit by a car while jay-walking dressed in head-to-toe gray out in the pouring rain, they would be exaggerating. I hope y'all know I joke about this incident because it actually scared the crap out of me. She was totally fine though, because it really was just a tap. Accidents happen—you gotta have a sense of humor about it, right?

You know, when we feel afraid, shaken up, or nervous, it really helps that we can open our mouths and speak life over ourselves. That day it was just reassurance from my daughters and myself that I was okay and everything was okay. It might sound simple, but try it out sometime. You can think happy thoughts, but power lies in the tongue, so let your thinking become your speaking when you need some uplifting. . .or reassurance that you didn't just run anyone over too bad. We need to be as quick to speak life as we are to word-vomit our negativity. Have you ever noticed that the further you get from God, the more negative you become? Easily offended, quickly angered, a little rude, constantly complaining. Maybe a little irrational? The words coming out of your mouth and the tone of your voice are evidence of what's going on in your heart. The power of life and death is in the tongue. What do you speak over yourself and others? Do you allow the strongholds within your thoughts to come out of your mouth? Or do you proclaim the promises you've been made? Fear is what the enemy feels when you say who you belong to. Reverse it on him. Push the fear he tries to place in your mind back in his face by telling him what you know. Jesus is your Savior; His Spirit is your guide. God is your Father, and you have favor. Preach it and believe it.

I've had to turn into Pastor Todd a time or two to keep myself from losing it. You ever have days you're so aggravated you need the stamina of a Southern Baptist preacher on a Sunday in order to speak life? Hey, do what you gotta do, girl. I can just picture you pacing around your kitchen all sweaty, arms waving, with the occasional stomp, and a flow of words from your spirit that take you an hour over the big church time limit. I had a day like this not too long ago. I had a solid two-hour cleaning frenzy in the bathroom. We have one full bathroom for this family of five. Four of those five are girls, so this isn't gonna work out in the long run. I scrubbed every inch of that bathroom. Hands and knees elbow grease kind of scrubbing. By the time I was done, I had sweated so much there was no way I was gonna pry my sports bra off later. When I finally finished, the whole bathroom sparkled. So I told everyone to stay out of there the rest of the day. Gotta poop? Dig a hole in the yard. Mama just cleaned.

Later that day I was resting in my room when I heard the dog whining. I could tell she was locked in a room because my four-year-old is always locking her in rooms by accident. Wanna guess which room she was stuck in? As soon as I opened the bathroom door, she sprinted out, and the odor of dog poo wafted out with her. Someone left a towel on the freshly scrubbed floor, so she made sure to poop on it as a favor to me. I started to walk across the bathroom to get some toilet paper for the poop, and I started slipping around everywhere.

Our Labradoodle has a beard, so when she drinks water or anything, it drips everywhere. This pup had been drinking out of the toilet, and to make things worse, she was drinking pee. My husband's pee. I know it was his, because for one thing, I know exactly what his pee smells like. If you don't know what your husband's pee smells like, are you even married? There's a very specific pungency to it. That and the fact there was no toilet paper. My girls make sure to use an entire roll when they go.

So I was slipping around on my husband's urine, trying to get dog poop out of a towel on the same floor I had just spent hours scrubbing. I wanted to scream. I angrily waddled out of the bathroom on my heels to see my husband napping on the couch. Watching him sleep peacefully while I hobbled around with his pee on my feet and dog poop on the floor had me feeling level-ten fury. I went over, flicked him on the forehead, and let him know the situation he had put me in. As I turned to finish cleaning up, I slid on a massive puddle of dog pee by the couch. I could not believe this was happening to me. So now I have dog *and* man pee on the bottom of my feet, poop stuck in a towel, and a bathroom I had just cleaned completely ruint. I sat on the side of my tub sweatin', hands wavin', occasionally stompin', and speaking words of life over myself as I washed my anger down the drain with all the urine coming off my feet. If you were listening at the door, you would have heard, "You are kind, you are a peace-keeper, you are slow to anger, *look at this mess*, deep breaths, Jesus in, anger out."

Then you wanna know what happened? I laughed. I truly believe laughter is one more way of speaking life. It helps you let out the bad, switch up perspective, and take your power back from overwhelming emo-tions. Sometimes we really need to speak life and laugh because crazy days are something we all go through, but very few of us talk about. If we can't laugh, we're likely to spew out our frustration in angry words. Which on the flip side, I'm also very good at. . .while driving. Based on what comes out of my mouth when I'm driving my car, I may need to check my heart. I guess calling people idiots at the four-way stop may be a sign I need to change the radio to the Jesus station. Although I still might accidentally call someone names right in the middle of "There is power in the name of Jesus—ya dingus!"

But nothing irks me more than the audacity of

someone going out of turn right there in front of everybody. Next thing you know, I'm driving down the road hatefully mocking how I imagine they must be. "Yeah, uh, I'm just gonna go ahead and go, because I don't have to take turns because I'm better than all of you. I don't have to wait in lines. Lines don't apply to me. Single-file lines, checkout lines, drive-through lines. I go straight to the front every time. I'm me, and y'all 're not." That is not exactly speaking life, is it? But have you found yourself spewing a lot of negativity in specific seasons of life?

We all have highs and lows, but they don't have to infect what we know to be true. I'm sure you've caught yourself saying things like *I can't, it's too hard, what if, I'm afraid,* or—one of the easiest words to say that we don't realize gets in our way—*but.* I think *but* might be one of the enemy's favorite words to plant right in the middle of every loving truth God says about you.

"God says I'm loved, *but* I don't really have any friends."

"Jesus says I'm worthy, *but* my family won't support me."

"Scripture says I'm never alone, *but* I feel like such an outsider."

"The Holy Spirit brings joy in the morning, *but*

alarm clocks don't bring me joy."

Unless we are complimenting our husband's rear end, let's try to keep from saying the word *but* when it's messing with our trust. The spot in your speech where that word used to be can simply be replaced with a period. Always speak what's true, and let God deal with insecurities that linger between your beliefs. Fear might give you the bubble guts, but the truth of God's Word is Pepto for the soul. Swallow it down before you word-vomit doubt all over the good plan in store for your life.

Let's keep it real here. Sometimes we vomit the wrong words before we gain control of our emotions. Who here has ever struggled in their marriage? Every single married person just raised their hand, and every lying married person needs to go ahead and schedule counseling to work on that whole faking nonstop love and adoration thing. Do you know how incredibly important it is to speak life over your marriage? Well, I know you know how hard it is to do that when he's driving a nail right through your nerves. There have been times when I was so angry with my husband that I said the most hurtful things I could think of. Even when I walked away to simmer down, I'd find myself going off

nanny to plant our garden while we're off shopping for our next Gucci bag, so we give our kids a store-bought pesticide apple with a side of Cheetos, *Karennnn.*"

Phew! Here's the thing: everyone needs to vent now and then. And kudos to you for utilizing the strength that only the Holy Spirit can provide to keep from killing Karen. (Sorry to all the kind Karens out there—your name is just fun for this kind of stuff.) But something I've learned about myself is that when my spiritual love tank is full, the words that flow from my mouth are life giving not life threatening, you know what I'm saying? This bottled-up, heart-racing, hot-blooded, furious *need* to "talk back," defend myself, or tell them like it is (even when it's just me by myself in the car looking crazy) is a sign that I'm personally in need of some time with God. Spouting off angry thoughts to myself for the purpose of being hateful in private instead of public is still me being hateful. If what I'm saying wouldn't be said in front of them, then it shouldn't be said in front of me either. For one thing, I'm not alone. Ever. I'm still in God's presence. He knows everything I'm thinking and feeling, and He is there to listen, guide, and replace the anger with peace. But when I speak it, y'all, when I *speak* it, I hurt my own heart. Even worse, I give the enemy something to work with. Thank goodness that when we find our temper tested, there are so many scriptures at our fingertips to keep us tongue tied. Here's one to read out loud as a reminder of what is right.

I absolutely love Isaiah 55:10–11. Read it slowly and think on it.

> "The rain and snow come down from the heavens and stay on the ground to water the earth. They cause the grain to grow, producing seed for the farmer and bread for the hungry. It is the same with my word. I send it out, and it always produces fruit. It will accomplish all I want it to, and it will prosper everywhere I send it."

This scripture really lays out the importance of what we speak over ourselves, others, and the atmosphere around us. Our words should plant seeds of value, feed a hunger for love, grow ourselves as well as others, and water what is good. Is what you've been speaking lately empty? Are your words hollow? Do they feed your faith or starve your spirit? Your words will accomplish the purpose for which you sent them out. What have you been achieving? If you say something with the intention to hurt someone, it will find a way to do so. Prime example: gossip. Oh goodness, this is gonna feel like a personal attack, because every one of us has partied hard at a good gossip get-together. Gossip is like chips and cheese dip. Hard to resist, easy to binge, and indulging too much will leave you feeling sick. Some of y'all are thinking, *Oh, but cheese dip is so good.* Well, gossip is tasty too, so y'all hush, you're gonna ruin the message. Gossip is sneaky. It can pop out of your mouth clothed as a concern for someone, an opinion of a situation, or even worse. . .a prayer request. Tammy at that church meeting waving her manicure like, "Oh Pastor Todd! I almost forgot, before we end our meeting, I just wanted all y'all to keep Miss Susie Lou in your prayers. I guess she had a 'Towanda' moment in the Piggly Wiggly parking lot when a lady banged her car with her buggy. I thought she seemed like she was struggling a little when she snapped at me during choir practice for a Facebook status she thought was about her. But that's neither here nor there, and I don't wanna gossip. We just really need to keep her in mind because she could use some bail and prayers, bless her heart." (In case you're not aware, Towanda is a character in the movie *Fried Green Tomatoes*. Do yourself a favor and watch it if you haven't.)

We give in to gossip for all kinds of reasons. It might be out of hurt feelings, a need for our side to be validated, a desire to be part of a group that spends a lot of time talking about people, or a lack of anything better to say in the midst of some awkward silence. But just like the scripture above says, your words will return to you having achieved the purpose for which you sent them. Meaning there's no such thing as getting away with the hurtful things you say. I can't tell you how many times I've been a little too open with my feelings about someone only to feel regretful and worried that it might get back to them somehow. Guess what—it almost always does. You know why? Because people who like to gossip with you will gossip about you. A Chatty Cathy ain't happy unless she's stirring up trouble in everybody's business. Be wary of someone in your circle who can't stop spewing negative things about others. If you join them, you'll find yourself wrapped up in hurting others while damaging your own personal peace. I have always said that a sign of spiritual maturity is a person's ability to know when it's best to just stay silent. When a woman has a spirit of peace about who she is, what she's doing, and what her future holds, there just isn't any desire to chirp with the birds who choke on their words. When you're full of joy, your words will reflect it. When you know who you are and what your purpose is, the faults of others don't interest you. Helping them along their journey does. You speak life over others, or you just zip it and give it to God. It is so hard sometimes. We are never going to like everyone, and we certainly don't have to support people we don't agree with, but bad-mouthing them is a choice.

To be honest, I know a person who makes my skin crawl. The mention of their name pokes at my gag reflex. I could spend hours venting about them. And until I get to a point where it's not so hard to let go of my feelings toward them, until they no longer have any influence over my gag reflex, until I find myself so focused on my own purpose that there's zero room for negative speaking about what someone else is doing, I know I have more growing to do. I have a long way to go, as I'm sure many of you do too. So we just need to keep learning and growing into who we are in Christ and into the purpose we're serving in this life, protecting our peace along the way.

Recycle the truth so it continues to come back to you. Let God's Word fill your thoughts, and let those thoughts bounce from your tongue to your ears, taking them in again and again until the cycle of what you know to be true about you is no longer vicious due to the sounds of loving repetitions. Speak life over and over, because words are your armor and you are a soldier, guarding your heart from the lies of the destroyer.

We know that a woman who speaks life must be brave. Planting seeds takes courage, and words of hate are always afraid.

Humble yourselves before God. Resist the devil, and he will flee from you. (James 4:7)

Have you ever felt like you've just been under attack? There have been seasons when I felt a heavy presence weighing on me. For the past year I've felt like the enemy was really on me mentally, emotionally, and spiritually. I felt a lot of stress, pressure, and difficulty surrounding my writing. Just this week I was visiting my mom in Alabama with my kids for a last trip of the summer, but also so I could get some time alone to work on this book. The night we arrived, I was having trouble falling asleep as usual, so I put on a "going to sleep prayer" from an app on my phone called Abide. I drifted off, listening to the soothing acoustics of a guitar underneath a deep prayer for peace, forgiveness, and rest. I have always had pretty lucid, vivid dreams—which makes the scary ones even more terrifying. But on this night the dream didn't just feel like a nightmare; it felt like a physical attack. I was sitting next to a little boy, but he wasn't a boy. He was looking at me with such intense hatred that I could feel my heart starting to race, and I wanted to get away from him. I attempted to get up, and his fingers stretched out and went right through my chest. I could feel it, and I was in that space of sleep where you're still dreaming but fully aware of yourself sleeping in bed. I began trying really hard to fully wake up, and when I opened my eyes, I could still feel my body jumping the way it did when his swordlike hands reached through my chest. I took a deep breath, put my hands on my chest, and rolled over to just go back to sleep. The dream picked right back up where it left off. Now his face was right in front of my face, telling me to say something. At first he was just looking me in the face and speaking in a low, angry voice, but then he quickly stood over me and began screaming for me to say something. He put the tips of his sharp fingers on my cheeks and was shaking my head back and forth. I opened my eyes, still feeling like he was holding my face, and my head shook side to side one more time before I sat up out of breath, sweating and terrified. Of course, I just kept saying to myself it was just a really bad dream.

But as I lay there, I couldn't help feeling like I had just been confronted with something evil. Something that really hated me. I honestly wanted to go crawl into bed with my mom, but then I remembered what this book is about, faith over fear. So I opened my mouth and reminded the enemy who I belong to. I said out loud, "I belong to Jesus Christ. I have His spirit within me, and I am not afraid." I put the prayer back on my phone, fell fast asleep, and slept in peace the rest of the night. These kinds of encounters make many people uncomfortable, and that's okay. But make no mistake, the enemy is real.

When you are growing in your walk with Jesus and choosing to walk in His purpose for you, there will be attacks from the enemy. That should only give breath to the sparking flame in your spirit to continue trusting in the Lord. When confronted with a spirit of negativity, hatred, or fear, open your mouth and speak life. Say it. The power of life and death is in the tongue, so when the enemy tests your faith, spit words of life in his face.

She laughs, unafraid of the enemy's lies. When he tries to speak death, she will choose to *speak life*.

Chapter 4

———— 888 ————

SHE FAILS

My health may fail, and my spirit may
grow weak, but God remains the strength
of my heart; he is mine forever.
PSALM 73:26

One time I decided to surprise my girls with a trip to the movie theater after school. I was having one of those days when I just wanted to remind them what an awesome mom they have. We loaded up on popcorn and candy, handed in our tickets, and made our way to theater six. As we waited for the previews to start, I stared at their excited faces, feeling extra good about myself. Wow, I really mother-crushed it today, and they are never going to forget this. The lights went down and the virtual popcorn roller coaster began. The next thing I knew, a preview started to play an opening scene of a woman standing in the rain facing the other way. As the camera zoomed in on her closer and closer, my arm made its way across both my girls' faces. Then the woman whipped around with half her face eaten off, and to make it five trillion times worse, she was holding a little baby. A *zombie* baby. I. Was. Appalled.

My oldest daughter had sunk so low into her chair it was almost folded up shut, and my middle was eyes wide open trying to knock my hand off her forehead so she could see. I was looking around the theater wondering if I was the only one ticked off that they were showing previews like that before a kids' movie. Nobody else seemed fazed. I straight panicked through three scary previews, thinking the theater had made a huge mistake, when it dawned on me that we might be in the wrong room. Right about that time, terrifying music boomed right through us as creepy red letters popped onto the screen, revealing to this awesome mom that she had her babies about to watch *The Conjuring*. Oh. Nope nope nope. I jumped up quick and ushered my traumatized daughter and her intrigued sister out the door as fast as I could in front of the other fifteen people who were in there. In my defense, some people had kids, or preteens, or whatever, with them. Our door was side by side with *The Conjuring* theater door, and I took the wrong one, pretty much ruining all their fun. One daughter couldn't get over me subjecting her to that horror, while the other was mad because she wanted to watch it. To this day, I can't take them to the movies without my oldest reminding me at least seven times to pay attention to what theater we go into. Looking back, I bet the other adults in that theater probably wondered why the heck I'd bring my two little girls to that movie. I had an awesome mom fail that day. I just tucked it into my book of never-ending oopsie stories. But these aren't really the kind of fails we fear, are they?

FAILURE TO DISCERN

Laughter isn't just what happens when your friend smashes her face into the super-clean JCPenney window instead of walking through the open door right next to it. I mean, I can still remember the hollering that came out of my body as I watched her stare confused and angry at that window before looking around at everyone like, *Can you believe somebody put that there?* with her faceprint still fresh on the glass behind her. Okay, fine, it wasn't a friend. It was me. It was my face smoosh story, and I had no friend there to witness it. I wish I would have though, because the walk of shame to my car afterward would have been less embarrassing with a friend. Thank goodness when we can't see the window coming for our face, God gifts us with an ability to see the humor in the aftermath of our humiliation.

Discernment sure can be tricky when the right path

doesn't seem as crystal clear as the wrong one. Life can feel like the house of mirrors in a carnival attraction at times. I took my girls through one recently, thinking it wouldn't be hard for me to see the way out since I'm a grown woman. But after walking into the third clear wall, I got a little scared to take another step. I had to slow down, look closely, and put my hands out to feel for the right path before stubbing my toe on another wrong one.

Y'all ever walk your rosy cheeks right into the wrong relationship? I've smashed my face on some glass a time or two, blindly stepping toward a nice smile and a few yummy compliments. Dang near broke my nose over a muscular forearm. Isn't it funny how we can leave a faceprint on the warning right in front of us and still bounce off it looking for another way in? Sometimes it takes a broken heart to realize a better path set before us.

Failing to recognize the right door to walk through could have some scary consequences, and we do feel afraid sometimes that we are making a mistake. There are a lot of wrong doors out there that look just like the door we were looking for. You're going to walk through and into the wrong ones from time to time. If you're like me, you might even charge through them like a wrecking ball now and then. But we know that God works for the good in all things, so whatever mistakes you're about to walk into will serve as a guide for your future "what not to dos." Don't let the fear of failing to discern keep you from taking steps forward. Embrace the face smash. As you move forward, you can laugh looking back.

FAILING TO MEET EXPECTATIONS

The definition of *fail* is to fade away or weaken, fall short, disappoint, or leave undone. You are most definitely going to do all of that if you are out there living, learning, using your voice, and growing. We all agree that nobody is perfect, so what's with being scared of disappointing others? A major reason for fearing failure is that you won't meet people's expectations of you. I played softball in college. I remember one game when we had bases loaded and two outs, and I was up to bat. I started letting thoughts of what everyone expected of me swirl around and drown out every ounce of confidence I usually carried with me into the batter's box. The next thing I knew, I'd taken a swing at a ball so far over my head I had to jump for it, gone golfing for another, and let a perfect pitch go right down the middle while

I stood by frozen. Three pitches, three strikes, game over. That's what a fear of failing others does—it robs you of everything you know you are capable of. I lost faith in my ability to perform. It didn't matter that I was prepared, ready, and able, because all of my focus had shifted to how horrible letting everyone down would feel. Pressure to please others will have you taking swings at all the wrong things and standing by frozen as opportunities pass you by.

Faithful woman, you were created to step up to the plate and crush it. The enemy knows it. Practice makes perfect, so put expectations aside and put to good use what God says about you. Every time you study the truth, praise the sacrifice made for you, and deepen your trust through Christ of what you are capable of, you strengthen the skill of choosing faith over fear. Your focus on the path set before you will begin to outweigh what anybody else has to say.

You can trust that God has placed a calling on your life. If you have faith to pursue it, there will always be people who can't see it. Living according to other people's expectations will weaken the purpose for which you've been created. If your purpose is weakened and it begins to fade, isn't that the definition of failure? Leaving this earth when your time comes with a calling left undone sounds much scarier than disappointing people.

There's no joy in pleasing everyone else at the expense of your peace. You can do what God says you can do, so if you keep showing up, you'll keep growing into everything He says you are—which is greater than any expectation a person can place on you.

There will be days we inevitably do or say things that people will judge us for or things that we regret. That's just being human. We make mistakes, lose our temper, forget to be thankful, yell at our kids, gossip, lose perspective, or resent our husbands for showering so quickly. (But seriously, it annoys me that he can get in and out so fast while I gotta wash, shave, shampoo *and* condition, run out buck naked to see what the bloodcurdling scream was about, jump back in after discovering it was over a Barbie shoe not fitting, get out and lotion my whole entire body, and then get pooped on when I'm done. I can't lie—there are days he hops in and out fresh as a daisy and I glare hatefully and then slam every cabinet in the kitchen. Sorry for that. Forgive me and my hormones, Lord.)

We will never be good enough for the standards of different kinds of people, from different backgrounds, with different views on life. We didn't used to have so many opinions shoved in our faces each day. Mamas, wives, sisters, single ladies, let me ask you. . .*What does God say about you?* Have you gotten so wrapped up in the differing opinions of other people that you can't hear the whispered words of the Lord? Well, snap out of it! Tune them out and tune Him in. It's as simple as that. He can be found offline, off the radar, off the map, away from the distractions of all the chatter. When you and the world are apart, He is right there inside your heart.

FAILING TO FAIL

Once you've succeeded, you've set a standard, and that can be scarier than the ease of failure. If you fail to fail, you just might realize everything you didn't know you could do—and now there's no excuse. How many times have you decided not to give your best effort because if there's a chance you could fail, you'd rather know deep down that you weren't really trying? Ope! I feel like I just personally attacked my own self. Hopefully that's a gut check for you too. The idea of failing while giving your very best effort may be the reason you're scared to set a higher standard. When we go bowling and I somehow can't get my warped ball out of the gutter, that's when I make sure everyone knows the lanes are tilted, my wrist hurts, and I'm just here to have fun. I wasn't really trying anyway. Lies! Oh yes, I was trying. I've rolled plenty of strikes before, which makes it even harder to stomach when I throw the ball right into the gutter. Deep down I desperately want to beat my husband for once in my life before I die. Gutter balls are way more bitter when you know how to roll like a winner. I want to hear the thunder as the pins crack and fall, not the lonely sounds of a slow-motion gutter ball. That's just embarrassing.

One time our whole family went bowling, and we were all excited to watch my brother-in-law roll his first strike of the night because he is basically a professional. He was in a league and had his own fancy ball with its own fancy ball bag and everything. By the time he got his wrist guard on, stretched his legs, cracked his neck, and tucked his custom-ordered ball-wiping towel into his back pocket, we were all anxiously at the edge of our seats, ready to witness Thor bring down the hammer like never before seen at the Bowling Stones family fun center. With a look so sharp it could cut through butter, he lined himself up and began his approach graceful as a giraffe on ice. As he reared back, about to bring the ball forward, his shoe decided it no longer wanted to play today, screeching to a halt and sticking to the floor while the rest of his body continued to fly forward. I haven't seen a belly slide that painful since I gave myself whiplash last summer showing my kids how to slip 'n' slide because they weren't doing it right. For a minute I thought his head might make it down the lane to the pins before his ball did. When I tell y'all I died laughing, I mean I genuinely feared for my life. I laughed so hard I went completely silent aside from sounds of muted breathless wheezing. I had to stop, drop, and roll on the floor just to try to catch my breath. That might have been too much failure for him to handle if he didn't have such a great sense of humor. The gift of laughter will catch you when you fall, cancel out fear, and restore faith to try again. Even after an epic fail, he still ended up beating us all in the end.

You see, the fear isn't of failing; it's of rolling gutter balls when you know you're capable of strikes. It's of falling short of the standard you set for yourself. Have you ever considered that it's not failure you're afraid of? Maybe you're afraid of the possibility of success. Failing leaves room to grow. But maintaining success? Phew, that can feel terrifying. Now that you know what you're capable of, you may question if you can keep this up. The pressure to hold yourself to that higher standard can create a lot of anxiety. For me, having God show me over and over what He's capable of in my life was really scary, because I started to fear I'd inevitably mess it all up.

Every time I speak in public, whether it's a serious or comedy event, I have a moment of complete terror that my first successful show was a fluke and I'm not actually capable of doing this well. Essentially, I have to keep showing God that I trust Him by taking that first step onto the stage anyway. When I think about the worst that could happen, it looks like me walking out in front of a bunch of people and going completely blank, running off the stage, blowing future opportunities, and disappointing everyone who put the event together, everyone who bought tickets, and everyone who ever believed in me. But if I let this fear keep me from a calling that is undoubtedly on my life, then I'd be placing it above faith that I can do all things Christ has called me to. Same goes for you. What's the worst that could happen? That's what my best friend always says when I'm feeling fear and stress.

At the end of the day, one thing will never ever change. You are loved. You have gifts and purpose. Most important, you cannot fail the One who matters most when you're taking steps toward your calling in faith. Even when you fail to meet a standard, His strength when you're weak is showing you what to learn in failure. Success isn't so scary when you understand that some failures are necessary in order to achieve it.

STEP BACK

Sometimes, all you need is discernment and peace. Discernment to make the best call regarding the path Christ has for your life and peace with the decisions you feel guided to make. Accept that you will make some mistakes. If you've been feeling restless and stressed, maybe it's time to log off, step away from the crowd, and shut down the voices of others. Just for a while. Just long enough to breathe, think, reconnect, and pray. Long enough to shake off the world and put on the armor of the Lord. Long enough to remember the truth. You are enough for your family, your friends, your job, and your gifts. You love enough. You give enough. You kiss and hug enough. You discipline enough. You make mistakes, and you're given grace. You're not alone in feeling like you're all alone. Nobody has it all together. Your loved ones, your friends, your coworkers, and even your enemies are yours for a reason. The mistakes you make will teach them as much as they teach you.

Remember and trust that God knows you, and He knows your future. With His guidance, discernment, mercy, and grace, you will do what is right by your purpose in life. Even your mistakes have already been developed for the good of those you love, and also for the good of those you don't even know. Look to the Word for assurance. Let it be your compass and just do the best you can. Let go of the judgment, guilt, and shame placed on you by others. Condemnation is not from God but from the enemy. God will convict you of changes you need to make with love and guidance, but the enemy will try to paralyze you with shame and doubt. Keep your eyes open for that deception. Remember, there's a difference between condemnation and conviction.

Have you ever noticed that when you fail a test, the problems you missed are forever burned into your brain? I will never again misspell Wed-nes-day or Feb-ru-ary. Getting it all wrong is a pretty efficient, long-lasting method for getting it right. There's no greater motivator to learn and do better than feeling like you've let someone else or yourself down. But you're given grace and forgiveness, so don't stand still. Sometimes we take a leap of faith and fall short because there's more to be learned from starting at the bottom and making the climb. If the fear of failure begins to hold you back, you're lacking trust. It's okay to feel it, but don't let it keep you from trying to succeed. Feel the fear as you make the jump. The Lord is your strength to get back up.

Here is reality. . .God is good. God has a plan for you, and God has a plan for me, failures included. I have a home now despite plenty of days in the past calculating how to continue affording our tiny apartment. I have three amazing little girls who are happy and love me endlessly despite plenty of tears shed over fears I could never provide them a good enough life. I have a husband who loves me even though he's seen the worst of me, and I still haven't quite figured out how to fully love and be loved. In the past I have failed in so many ways every single day, and my future has always turned out okay.

As you're reading this today, you're okay too. If not

now, you will be. You are capable of recovery. A new day of victory awaits, so always keep your faith. I know what tragedy feels like. Losing my niece to cancer changed my perspective toward life and toward failure. I have what matters most to me. Everything else is gravy. Embarrassment passes. Feelings fade. You live and you learn from mistakes. Remember that the next time the fear of failing threatens to keep you from the possibility of success.

Being saved means you are forgiven by the only One who matters, the only One who truly knows who you are to the core of your soul. So ask for grace, apologize when necessary, and do not compare yourself to anyone. If you are trying your best not to walk the beaten path but to be better, that is amazing and you can always start fresh. God can't be strong in your weakness, sister, if you're trying to be perfect all the time. You're doing it wrong, and He will make it right.

WHEN WE FAIL, GOD'S GOT US

We try to be strong. So much stronger than we are capable of. How many times have you repeated to yourself, "I can do this. I can do this"? But when you lean on your own ability, that's when doubt takes over. Which turns out to be necessary in order for you to see that you need His strength. I can do all things through Christ who strengthens me (Philippians 4:13). He strengthens me because I'm weak. Like 2 Corinthians 12:9 reminds us, His power is made perfect in our weakness—not in our already perfect strength. So if you feel like failing makes you weak, consider it a catalyst to getting stronger. It's so simple, yet we still give the fear of failing power over our faith some days.

It boils down to trust. Failure is inevitable. Do you trust that when you do fail, God's got you? When I fail, He pulls me through. A kind word, an apology, a new path, an opportunity opened when a different door closes, a chance to make a difference through a valuable lesson learned, or a much-needed release through laughter when relief is needed. These are all a part of growth. These are the ways He pulls me through. Failure bears good fruit too. Life is full of disappointments because people always make mistakes—and that includes you. Yet nothing can change what God sees in you. You are capable of failing over and over again, yet still being successful. As long as you have breath in your body, there's a plan for your presence. Don't let overwhelming feelings steal that truth from you. Peace is around the corner, because God's plans for you are good. The moments you fail don't change that. As long as you believe something good is ahead, you can overcome your fears of failing to do good work in the future.

She doesn't laugh in the face of failure because she isn't afraid. She is freaking out sometimes. The pressure can really get to her. Right now, she is me. I had a full-blown anxiety attack in the middle of writing this chapter, because I'm scared to death to fail in every way I just spoke of. I'm scared my writing will fall short; I'm afraid to disappoint; I'm terrified of the pressure of a deadline. I'm so tired. I want you to know with tears and short breaths that I can barely catch, I know it's not easy to overcome a fear of failing. I feel like crawling under a rock and shutting everyone out right now. But I'm gonna type it out anyway. Because despite how terrified I feel right now, I know that at the end of the day, it's going to be okay. Everything is going to be okay. None of this is easy; fears are very serious. They can overwhelm your body and your mind. They can make you sick and drain your joy. It happens. We laugh later on, because as scared as we are now, ultimately it will be all right. A deep breath and a lifted weight aren't far away. So stick it out. It's worth every failing day to finish what you start.

In John 13:7 Jesus said, "You don't understand now what I am doing, but someday you will." Trust that every failing moment serves a purpose. You might not know what it is just yet, but when the time is right, you will.

She laughs without fear of failure because she knows in time, He'll reveal His purposes.

Chapter 5

She's Humbled

Above all else, guard your heart,
for everything you do flows from it.
PROVERBS 4:23 NIV

Some of y'all never had to flush an overflowing toilet by pouring water out of a gallon jug into the tank, and it really shows. More than once when I was young, we had to use the neighbor's hose pipe to fill up a milk jug with water so we could get rid of a day's waste, brush our teeth, or wash off with a damp cloth. I tell my mama all the time how much I really appreciate knowing what it's like to struggle. But when I was a kid, I fantasized nonstop about having more money. Publishers Clearing House owned the majority of my daydreams.

One time I checked the mail and found an envelope from them that said "You Have Won!" My eyes bugged out, because Mama had a friend who said she had the gift of prophecy, and she told her we had a bigger home, more money, and a man for my mom to marry in our near future. I didn't care for the man part much, but the money part had me wanting to believe her. When I ripped open this letter, I thought, *Thank You, God—the crazy prophecy lady was right after all!* I read every single last detail in the terms and conditions, and I'm telling y'all, it said we won. I took off running up and down the road through our neighborhood waving the envelope through the air and yelling, "We won! We won a million dollars. We are rich! We're moving to the rich neighborhood. God heard my prayers! The prophecy lady was right!" Back and forth in front of our house, I skipped, jumped, and giggled uncontrollably. My mom, sister, and brother came out to see what the heck I was goin' on about. My mama was shaking her head and laughing but also getting a little annoyed and embarrassed. She hissed at me, "Git in the house. Git. In. The. House. Yellin' like a lunatic, you're scaring the neighbors. Pick up the rest of the mail off the ground and come inside." I was like, "We don't even need these bills, Mama. Alabama Power can kiss our butts. We can buy Alabama Power. How 'bout we'll shut *their* lights off."

I sprinted in out of breath like Charlie from Willy Wonka, waving my golden ticket around. I begged and begged my mama to please just fill it out and mail it in. She wasn't having it. She kept telling me it wasn't real, it was a scam, I was wasting my time. I was so upset. All she had to do was fill out the letter and mail it back in, and we could have been millionaires. To this day, I still feel like maybe we could have been the next Publishers Clearing House family on a commercial getting a knock on the door. I could see it all playing out in my mind, them standing there with blue balloons and a huge cardboard check as I opened the door with wide eyes, followed by my mom coming to the door like, "Who is it?" and me turning to her and saying, "I told you, I told you!" Then I'd forever be known in my family as the one responsible for saving us from poverty. Therefore, my mom *had* to let me hire New Kids on the Block to sing at my birthday party. If any of my middle school classmates ever wondered what I was dreaming about that had me drooling so much on my desk, this is it.

I may come from humble beginnings, but the experience of having next to nothing created a real issue for me in regard to humility. It's probably the *most* important characteristic I want to live with, yet the hardest to maintain. That may sound strange, because in many ways my Goodwill upbringing absolutely instilled a sense of gratitude for what I have and an awareness of what my family truly needs to be happy. Which is not material things. But on the other hand, I developed a pretty hardened heart toward anyone who might "look down" on me. We often experienced judgment, ridicule, and stares rolling around in our hoopty station wagon, wearing donated clothing, and writing checks from overdrafted accounts. So I became almost hyper-determined not to be looked down on. Watching my mama struggle to take care of us, exhausted and desperate, I really became angry toward my dad. Which crossed over into resentment toward men. *All* men. I started to develop a pride that served as a wall around vulnerability. *I don't need anybody to take care of me. I take care of myself. I know who I am. I know what I need. I know what I'm doing.* Fear of humiliation began to overwhelm any traces of humility. With that attitude, I obviously wasn't able to grow and mature the way we need to if we really want to serve our calling.

Being humble is crucial to becoming more like the woman who *laughs without fear.* Don't confuse it with being weak or soft. It takes so much more strength to live each day with a humble heart than to bulldoze through life driven by pride. Six characteristics of a humble heart can give you a joyful spirit and the freedom to laugh without fear of what the future has in store. If you are content, grateful, patient, teachable, hard to offend, and dead to yourself, you'll find extraordinary joy in being humble.

CONTENTMENT

In my season of life building an at-home fitness business, I dove into personal development. Everyone can benefit from pumped-up guidance and encouragement. Spunky self-help books and materialistic-driven motivational speeches that repeatedly call you *sister* will really get you riled up, believing that if you just work harder, hustle faster, and make more sacrifices, you can have it all, lady boss babe. And *sister*, you can. But if everything you have isn't giving you peace, maybe you've forgotten that having a heart for Jesus means being thankful you have all you need.

Working in network marketing as long as I did, the drive to succeed was drilled into my brain. I kept thinking if I just worked harder, stayed up later, woke up earlier, and pushed every day, it would be worth it for the financial freedom and success I was after. But about five years into it, I found myself having sacrificed all my happy in the hustle of trying to prove to everyone around me that I could do it all. I had lost myself to the stress of success. I was so busy trying to catch up to the lifestyles of others in my company that success became more about status and money and less about joy and family.

Comparison and jealousy are the enemies of humility. When you're all wrapped up in working hard for the glory of yourself instead of the glory of God, you can't see the beauty in everything right in front of you. This is where I was at mentally and emotionally when I got the phone call saying that my niece had cancer. And then—*bam*—just like that, the reality of what matters so much more than anything else brought me to my knees. It wasn't until I found myself broken and humbled that I was able to really connect with the Holy Spirit. For the first time in years of hustle, I felt filled with peace and an understanding that when my heart was in the right place, I'd find relief from the stress of success. When I'm following the path God has set before me, for the purpose of glorifying Him through the good works He has prepared for me to do, I'll feel deep contentment along the way. I can be present and rest in the knowledge that I have everything I need and will be given more if it's His will. That's humility. You put His will first, no matter what, because you trust that He knows what you don't, and He works for your good always. Even when you don't get what you thought you needed, or wanted, or so desperately prayed for. You have a deep-seated faith that when the time is right, He will show you why.

Coming from nothing, all I could think of was wanting to show everyone that I was more than my circumstances. I wanted a bigger home, a nicer car, vacations, and freedom to relax. I thought I would be happy if I could give my kids double what I had growing up. Even if it meant giving them the tired, stressed-out, aggravated version of me, because that's just what you gotta do. Work hard now, play hard later. But that's not what *my children* want from me. They don't need nice things; they just want me. The best of me. They want me to be happy, silly, and content with time spent doing absolutely nothing with them. I am not saying don't work hard. I am not saying there's anything wrong with sacrifices in pursuit of your passion. I'm saying, make sure your passion is driven by Jesus' calling on your life, not by accumulating material things at the expense of precious time with those who matter most.

Stay grounded in contentment with what you have as you work for whatever it is God has placed on your heart. Contentment is not complacency; it's appreciation for everything you are so blessed to have. It's trusting that if you follow God's path for you with patience, loving God and loving others along the way, you'll have more than you ever knew you wanted, and what you want will be so much more valuable than money, houses, or cars. Excess isn't necessary when you walk with the Lord. There is so much peace in simplicity. A humble heart is soaked in gratitude, content with whatever God provides.

GRATITUDE

Gratitude goes hand in hand with humility. An attitude of gratitude is often a matter of perspective. When I was young, all my focus seemed to be on what I *didn't* have. So when all these people around us were helping us get by, their generosity went right over my head. The church fed us, clothed us, and even helped us to get a car at one point. I saw a crappy, embarrassing clunker when I should have seen an answered prayer. Had I been grateful, I may have actually allowed their generosity to fuel a good deed paid forward on my part. Maybe you've heard the old tale of a man who stumbled upon a lion with a thorn stuck in its paw. The man gently removed the thorn. Later on, the man was captured and thrown into a den with a starving lion—the same beast he'd helped before. The lion licked his hand and spared his life. Gratitude and humility serve the good of others first, and as a result, good things come back in return.

Some of the smallest sentiments of kindness had the biggest impact on my life. The old softball glove I received from my mom's church friend rippled right into the scholarship that got me through college. And I just took it begrudgingly, irritated that I couldn't have a nice new glove like everyone else. Having a strict mama, one who cared enough about me not to let me get away with doing stupid things unpunished, gave me a sense of value. Her discipline may have been annoying at the time, but at least I knew she believed I was worth doing better. I used to wish so bad that I had a cool mom who would just let me do what I wanted. I basically wished she cared less. But what I had was an exhausted, stressed, flat broke, hickory switch–slinging mama who would drop everything and sprint down the street to me the moment someone said I was hurt. Yup. I said sprint. Like on her feet.

We were playing popcorn on my friend's trampoline down the road. This was back before safety nets kept our fragile babies from possibly getting a scratch on their poor wittle elbows. . .or breaking their arm in half. My brother and another neighborhood boy would jump at the same time and bounce me as high as they could. I got ricocheted clear off that springy death mat all the time. But this time, my body landed on top of my left arm, which landed across a broomstick. I thought I must've snapped the broom in half when I heard a loud crunch underneath me. But when I stood up and realized my left hand was stuck in the "walk like an Egyptian" dance move position, I knew something was wrong. I pulled my sleeve down to my elbow to see that my forearm was snapped in half, shaped like a triangle with the bone almost poking through the front of my favorite tickle spot. Everyone screamed, looked at each other, and screamed some more. I took off in an adrenaline-fueled dash toward home, holding my arm in front of my terrified face and yelling, "I don't wanna die!" You know how dramatic ten-year-olds are.

My friend's dad came out, yelling for me to come back and quit running before I tripped and ripped my arm clean off. He called my mom, and I suppose it's in a mama bear's genes to run straight to her cub at the sign of trouble, because as I was sitting on their porch trying not to hyperventilate, I looked up and saw my mother running down the street full speed ahead with pure panic plastered across her face. It's the same face people make when they accidentally fart in public. Shocked and a little mad about it. Now let me tell y'all, neither before this day nor any day since have I *ever* seen my mama run. She had to have hung up the call, untangled herself from the curly phone cord, and dashed out the door right past the car to get to her baby on foot so she could, I don't know, throw me over her shoulder and literally run me to the hospital. My point is, she loves me so much, she's irrational at the thought of anything happening to me. I don't have a mom who let me do whatever I wanted so I'd be her best friend. I have a mom who cared more about my safety and the kind of person I'd be. I didn't realize just how good I had it. I was too distracted wishing I had the kind of money, house, and life that others had to realize how rich I was with a loving mother.

We can waste a whole lot of our lives whining and complaining and feeling bitter over everything we don't have. Or we can appreciate what we've got while looking forward to whatever God provides us in His timing. A humble heart can walk with a joyful spirit, patient in faith and grateful for the fruits that have yet to be claimed in the future.

PATIENCE

One morning my youngest daughter, Bodie, asked me for a cup of milk. As I was pouring the cup of milk, she started whining at the top of her lungs, "Not meeeeyulk!" So I set a cup of water in front of her, which led to a teeny-tiny tot slowly sliding down out of her chair as she cried in despair because I didn't give her milk. I stood over her holding a cup of water and a cup of milk like, "So let me get this straight. You asked for milk, so I gave you milk. But you didn't want milk, so I gave you water. But you didn't want water, you wanted milk? You need a nap."

Sleepy toddlers aren't much different than impatient adults. Both need to slow down, take a breath, and chill. I once saw a meme reminding us about Elijah wanting to die in 1 Kings 1:19, and God basically gave him food and told him to rest. So you see, snacks and naps are scriptural. Humility doesn't rush God into giving us what we want when we want it. When we're humble enough to know that sometimes what we want isn't what we need, we can let the Holy Spirit guide us instead of our own flesh.

The terrible twos for toddlers is the stage of life when they are learning they can't always have immediate gratification. Shoot, sometimes they get what they asked for and then pitch a fit because they don't want it. Has there ever been a time in your life when you felt like you were on the verge of having a meltdown because nothing was going your way? Keeping the pace of those around you, striving to reach major goals, or hustling to meet unrealistic expectations can lead you to take on more than you're ready for. "God doesn't give you more than you can handle" is a popular phrase, but an impatient person will absolutely pile more onto their plate than they can handle.

Here's an example I'm not proud of. I do a fundraiser every year for Saint Jude in memory of my niece. Last year I felt an immense amount of pressure and anxiety over reaching our goal and raising more than the year before. The donations weren't coming in as fast as I wanted them to, and I started to get impatient. So I began offering way too many giveaways every week. Great for everyone wanting free stuff, but outrageously expensive for me. In an effort to do something good, I got swallowed whole by promises I couldn't afford to keep. But I was so antsy that I didn't even think about the cost. I offered too much of myself, freaked out, got anxious, and disappointed a lot of giveaway winners. Impatience almost always leads to mistakes. Had I been humble enough to appreciate what was coming in little by little, I wouldn't have tried rushing it and getting in over my head. But humility understands that the purpose of failure is to help us learn and be better. A humble heart waits patiently, knowing that God's timing is always better than ours. In the meantime, maybe just get a snack and take a nap.

TEACHABILITY

> *Pride leads to disgrace, but with humility comes wisdom.* (Proverbs 11:2)

> *You're not funny. You're ugly. You act like you're on drugs. You've changed. I hate when people get big online and then start wearing makeup; just be yourself. Pray you find yourself again. How could you have faith in a God that gave your niece cancer?*

These are just a few things said to me by complete strangers on social media. Seems like they come all at once when I'm trying really hard to bite my tongue and be humble enough to take the words of others as opportunities to learn and grow.

I don't know about you, but this one is tough for me sometimes. Humble people blossom so brilliantly into who they are created to be, because they aren't afraid to be deflated. A student mentality isn't too puffed up with pride to let God breathe new life into it. It's okay not to know everything, to mess up, to say the wrong thing, take something the wrong way, or have a misunderstanding. Those who embrace the perspectives, wisdom, and constructive criticism of others can make such a difference in the world, because they truly understand the relationship between mistakes and purpose. It isn't easy. I spent so much of my life feeling defensive, ashamed, and embarrassed because my family was poor, my dad wasn't around, and other kids made fun of me—not to mention the shame I experienced from being sexually abused when I was a child. (You may not have known about that part of my past. I wrote about it in my first book, *Odd(ly) Enough*, so without retelling the entire experience, I just want to let you know if you've experienced the same, you're not to blame, and it's okay to talk to someone.) So hearing others' critical comments tends to create an immediate reaction of anger, annoyance, and attitude. I don't even like telling y'all that, because my flesh is already trying to say, "Now people are gonna start criticizing you just to get a reaction." It wouldn't be the first time.

We live in the age of social media, where everyone

thinks they know pretty much everything about everyone. I was given a platform from my first viral video, and it has continued to grow. I choose to speak, share, and put content out there, knowing it will be criticized, because a year before the video sparked a following, God spoke into my broken heart that my purpose was to speak. As painful as it feels some days, I know He works on my humility through the online negativity. Sometimes people take digs at me that transport me right back to the defensive, hardened little girl who identified with all the wrong that had been done to her. In those moments, I want to lash out, feed into my anger, and set them straight. But deep down I know that my ability to handle meaningless words from strangers with grace is a reflection of my maturity in Christ.

Oddly enough, this platform I've been blessed with has put me in a position to allow the Holy Spirit to work on tearing down some of the deepest strongholds limiting my growth. Some days I pass the test, and my spirit feels joyful, knowing I reflected Christ with love and kindness. Other days I reply to a hateful comment with as many sarcastic GIFs as it takes to make them want to shove their hands through the screen and choke me. I won't lie: for a moment it feels really good to get back at someone who has been rude. But God. He always convicts me. I've actually sat like a scolded child before, saying to God, "Come on though, that was funny!" But even if He thought it was, I don't get away with it. It will bother me until I make it right, take it down, and admit I could have handled the situation better. That's what a growing spirit should do though. . .make your skin crawl. As you grow further from your emotions and strongholds, your flesh will have to let go of the ego and face your convictions. A person with a humble heart has no problem hanging their head to repent for mistakes and seek answers in prayer. The Holy Spirit teaches the deepest lessons from our messes.

DEFENSE AGAINST OFFENSE

Man, I wanna be hard to offend. The next time I'm minding my own business walking toward the tampons trying to remember what I came to the grocery store for and some stranger tells me to smile, I wanna continue shopping without having allowed their comment to steal my peace. But really this is just my face, and I clearly have Jesus in my heart if I manage to respond without being smart during the time of the month I have the least amount of control over my anger. These days we get plenty of chances to practice keeping our joy in the face of hurt feelings, don't we? There are so many reasons to strengthen our defense against offense. For one, we are trying to be teachable, and it's tough to press a lesson through the feelings of someone who is easily offended. Offense is like a parasite that overwhelms clarity and leaches away at peace. If it makes its way to your heart, it will eat away at your ability to live in the likeness of Christ. The closer you are to Christ, the more you live according to the Spirit and the less you live according to the flesh. So if you find yourself getting all worked up over someone's words, take it as an indicator that it's time to be still. Disconnect from the world for a bit so you can reconnect to God. I've found that people who are easily offended oftentimes misunderstand and manipulate a circumstance in order to justify offense. Because when they are offended, they can lash out and project anger built up over something they haven't confronted emotionally. Someone who is hard to offend has a heart that has been healed, with no pent-up distress just waiting to be triggered.

I mean, who wants to walk around with their pantaloons in a bunch all the time? I, for one, want to be happy. Humility provides the stability we need to live joyfully. Emotions, words, and circumstances don't control our behavior. Because we're rooted in the truth, we're slow to take offense.

I think what makes humility the central characteristic I want to build my life around is the fact that humble people try to do what is right for those around them, not just themselves. Jesus left us His Spirit to guide us down the path of loving God first and loving others second. We are here to serve others in such unexpected ways that they will see who lives in us. Ego, pride, inconsideration, selfishness, and arrogance aren't hard to find. But when we come across a story of incredible humility, our spirits are moved to tears. Why? Because we know humility goes against our human nature. It allows us to see the goodness of God shining brightly in the spirits of others and, even more, to have His goodness shining in our own lives as well. I want that. Don't you want that? To be a vessel?

I saw a story once about a homeless man who would spend every day begging for change so that he could take whatever he was given straight over to the women and children's shelter. He had absolutely nothing, but he never kept a dime. People like that are so rare. The goodness that flows from humility is so pure, so courageously vulnerable and dripping in faith. This goodness means knowing that nothing I do in my time here on earth will matter when I'm gone except for the way I show love to others. Yet it's so easy to get all caught up in making more money, having more stuff, being more successful, and gaining more popularity. Why is it so easy?

It's easy because it feels good. It is satisfying to our flesh to be the best and have the most. A puffed-up ego loves to be petted. The problem is, there's no room for conviction. Without conviction, we lack discernment. Without discernment, we miss opportunities to reach our full potential. There are no limits to the difference a woman called by Christ can make. But a shortage of humility puts a cap on your impact. Pride shuts down guidance, leaves zero space for mistakes, and fails to realize that if a person has no weakness, they'll never be able to embrace God's strength.

DEATH TO SELF

> Humble yourselves before the Lord, and he will lift you up in honor. (James 4:10)

I wasn't willing to let go of my need to succeed until my niece was diagnosed with cancer. When I came home from the hospital visit, I felt completely humbled by what I had seen. So much suffering among some of the most joyful little spirits. I returned home feeling heartbroken and inspired. Sitting alone in my car, for the first time in a really long time, I broke down and let go. That was the moment. The moment I truly felt the Holy Spirit.

Have you ever been so determined to make things work that you convince yourself you're fine while losing your mind? The pride of successfully being in control overwhelms even the most determined. Being humble means getting down low so you can lay it all out. We try so hard to keep our heads up that we forget the power found when we bow. In my own life I had to come to an absolute physical, mental, and emotional breakdown before admitting that I couldn't do life without God. Dying to myself has meant dying to control, dying to anger, dying to resentment, dying to distrust, dying to what feels good, and dying to what others want from me. A big part of wanting control was my disbelief that anybody else wanted what was best for me. I grew up with an "I can do it" mentality, because relying on others wasn't an option. But the day I died to my desire for control and all the strongholds connected to it, I felt a tremendous release in my spirit.

Every single day this world does its best to harden our hearts. To distract us from who we really are and what's really important. It's in the breakdown that we open up our spirits to the truth. We are nothing. Nothing without Jesus. He is love; He is grace; He is mercy; and He is humility. He represents what truly matters. You know why we are to love God and love others? Because the depth of love, beauty, strength, and power to change the entire world for the better lies within us where He resides. It is through Him that we experience the magnificence of what life was always intended to be. When we love Him first, we in turn tap into a love within ourselves that makes us capable of lifting others up. We die to ourselves so we can be the fullest version of ourselves. Which means laying down all our ego, all our pride, all our chains, all the control, and all the hurt and worry brought on by the world. When we humble ourselves, we can quit clinging to everything holding us back and finally relax, throw our heads back, and laugh. We can realize exactly what we've been called for, and even better, we'll finally be able to see the path to getting there. Hallelujah, yes, ma'am.

Pride is a side effect of pain. The enemy sneaks it in

disguised as strength so you don't realize your humility is fading away.

> *Pain: I hurt because my dad disappointed me.*
> *Pride: You don't need him or anyone else. Hold*
> *your head up.*

> *Pain: I hurt because my innocence was stolen.*
> *Pride: Never again does anyone deserve your*
> *trust. Hold your head up.*

> *Pain: I hurt because my peers made fun of me.*
> *Pride: Be better than them, whatever it takes.*
> *Hold your head up.*

Pride shouts, "Head up, shoulders back, take control, you're better than them, shove down the heartbreak, and show everyone how strong you are!"

It doesn't work. It doesn't work, because your hurts and whatever's causing them do not define you. You are not of the world. A spirit belonging to Christ isn't controlled by the flesh. Bow your head to Him instead of lifting it up to your ego, and He will hold you higher than the pain hiding behind your pride. You don't have to be afraid to admit that something within you needs to change. You can humble yourself and look back and laugh as you move into your future, free of worry that you might get hurt. All the pain from before has been taken from you, and you've been made new.

She laughs because her humbled heart carries no chains.

Chapter 6

─ 888 ─

SHE LISTENS

Those who listen to instruction will prosper;
those who trust the Lord will be joyful.
Proverbs 16:20

I got so lost on some country back roads the other day. I started off knowing exactly where I was going, but then I went straight when I should have turned, and next thing I knew I was taking a tour of Harvest, Alabama. I was visiting my mom and thought I'd finally figured out how to get everywhere I was going without using the GPS. So when I realized I'd gone a couple of miles in the wrong direction, my first thought was *I can figure it out*. After all, I could remember my mom, stepdad, and sister standing in a circle telling me the fastest route back to my mom's house. Let's see, it went something like this: *All you gotta do is take a right, a right, a left, and then another. No, just tell her to take Birch to Capshaw and Mapco is there. Why doesn't she just go down Old Railroad Road and look for the light after that barn—but if she sees the boiled peanuts sign, she's gone too far.* A thought popped into my head that maybe I should just pull over and use Mapquest, but naturally I decided to randomly turn down Nance Road instead and just see if I saw anything familiar. Problem was, every road was familiar. Because every single road had a Dollar General and a First Baptist Church, and I don't know how, but at every turn I saw the exact same cow. At least two more times the thought *Just pull over and use your navigator* crossed my mind. I ended up finding my way home, but it took way longer than it should have.

Have you ever completely ignored the whispering voice trying to give you guidance and wound up taking the long way home? That's okay. Regardless of the route you take, eventually when you listen, you will have learned some lessons along the way. The little detour I took taught me a few different routes to get back home, so I doubt I'll ever find myself lost again—at least not on those same back roads. Even if there is a deceiving clone of a cow on every route. We listen and we learn. But what really keeps me laughing is that even when I don't listen the first time, God keeps on directing. Just like when the Australian navigator voice keeps rerouting you right up until you pull into your destination. No matter how deeply lost you've found yourself, no matter how many wrong turns you've taken, no matter how far away you feel you are, God will never stop seeking you. All you have to do is listen.

The last year was the hardest year of my life.

It made no sense to me because so many good things were happening. I published my first book, *Odd(ly) Enough*. I performed my first comedy show, spoke at a couple of women's events, traveled to several book signings, and raised over forty thousand dollars for Saint Jude Children's Hospital in memory of my niece Ansley. I was living the dream, and from the outside, anyone would think my life was going pretty amazing.

But somewhere in the middle of all this, I found myself incapable of feeling happy. Something began to feel *off* with me. Every promise God made me continued to be fulfilled, but more and more days started to begin and end with me in bed feeling frustrated, down, anxious, or—worst of all—indifferent. I stopped taking care of myself completely. I mean, it's nothing new for me to go a few days without a shower. But I would go a week in the exact same clothes, not brushing my teeth, barely even speaking to my kids, and getting up only to use the bathroom or eat. The worst part about it was that on the inside, I was begging myself to just get up and be who I am. For hours I'd lay there thinking, *Just get up. Just put your feet on the floor. Go for a walk, take a shower, play with your daughters, get some groceries— please just do something. Anything. What is wrong with you?*

I started to feel trapped in my own mind, and then I started hating myself for it. I had just written an entire book around the freedom of knowing your identity in Christ, and here I was unable to break free of this unexpected mental battle. I just couldn't understand how I could be struggling like this when nothing about my faith had weakened. I knew better, but that wasn't changing this pit of negativity that I couldn't seem to shake. This went on for over nine months. Some days I'd feel like myself, and other days were a battle followed by frustration because I thought it had passed.

One evening I was standing in the kitchen cooking spaghetti and feeling so happy that I was actually cooking. My three girls were playing together, chasing each other, squealing, and giggling. I was stirring the sauce, when all of a sudden the sounds they were making really started to bother me. Every screech built more and more tension inside my chest. My head started to hurt, my heart started to race, and I began to feel panicky, like I was going to pop. Their feet hitting the floor, the in our family usually noticed their mental health take a turn. Stress, overwhelm, frustration, bad moods, PMS—those are all completely normal. Everyone feels those. But I knew deep down that what I was experiencing was different, and it was out of my control. I didn't want to be another person with anxiety or depression. It seems like everyone has one or the other, and the words get tossed around so often. I didn't want people to think I was just lazy or hadn't done enough personal development or prayed enough. The fear of what other people and other Christians might assume of me kept me second-guessing what the whisper of the Lord had been telling me for months: *Something is off. Talk to someone.*

Some Christians think if you are truly saved and have enough faith, you won't deal with these kinds of struggles. I'm gonna shout it from the rooftops: if you wouldn't blame a Christian's faith for the stomach flu, don't you dare attack them over a mental health struggle. I'd felt an urge to talk to someone, have some tests run, check my hormones and thyroid for a while, but I pushed it away, thinking it would get better if I just tried harder. I coached women for five years on personal development, self-care, mental health, and spiritual growth. I know how to take care of myself. If something is off in the regulation of your hormones or some other chemical imbalance, it's not something you can fix with some yoga any more than motivational speeches cure cancer.

This depression had crept up on me slowly over time, triggered by stress and overwhelm. Looking back, I started to realize that I'd been struggling with anxiety for years, but I always just brushed it off, not realizing what it was. When I was pregnant with my first daughter, I'd often get really dizzy and feel like I was going to pass out when we were at the store or in closed spaces around a lot of people. My heart would start pounding, I'd start sweating, and my vision would begin to blur. I'd have to get myself outside as quickly as I could to sit down and breathe. I thought this was just a pregnancy thing, but it actually happens to me fairly often when I'm in a closed space that's crowded. I don't know why, and it doesn't happen every time, but when it does, it comes over me fast and out of nowhere. I've always been a nail biter. Biting your nails is usually just a bad habit. But I do it uncontrollably when I'm under a lot of pressure. I bite and pick my thumbs until they bleed and throb; and I know it sounds weird, but I almost like the way the pain feels while I'm picking them. Later, when my anxiety has passed, they hurt like crazy, but at the time it's a weird but satisfying distraction from stress. I picked the skin off my thumb so much this last year that my phone doesn't even recognize my thumbprint anymore.

I don't understand how so many people refuse to recognize that your brain, your genetics, your cellular wiring, and your hormones are a physical part of your body—same as your bones. When I broke my arm in half that day falling off the trampoline, nobody discouraged me from getting a cast. It's what I needed to help heal my broken bone. So why would anyone discourage someone from talking to a therapist, having tests, and if needed, taking medication to help regulate whatever is *off* inside of them? Not everyone needs medication, but if you do, there is no shame in it. So many women like me avoid even making the phone call to set up an appointment out of fear of the ignorant things people might say. As if you're depressed because you aren't doing enough to fight it. I had a doctor advise me to just get back to exercising and eating well like I was before. I found it so disheartening, because if someone like me who has always taken care of herself and knows what to do and how to do it all of a sudden finds herself unable to get out of bed for reasons she can't explain, you can be sure it's not because she's just choosing not to. Trust me, nobody chooses to feel this way. But with that being said, if you find yourself feeling off, it is your choice to get help or not. It is up to you to trust your instincts, listen to the quiet voice in your heart, and reach out for help.

Christian women dealing with anxiety and depression, I want you to know it's not because you aren't a devoted enough servant. Yes, Jesus Christ gives us joy, peace, and healing in our spirit. He also gives us discernment, understanding, and guidance. So if it's the unseen within your body giving you trouble despite your faithful heart, there is nothing wrong with letting Him guide you to someone He has gifted with the ability to help you. Trust your instincts, and listen to His voice over people who do not understand.

In my struggle, all I could think about was wanting to feel like myself again. The way I had felt the year before. The idea of possibly needing medication in order to feel a way that is supposed to just come naturally made me so angry. I didn't want this to be a part of my story. My story already involved poverty, sexual abuse, family addictions, and tragic loss. Why couldn't I catch a break from mental health struggles? Well, probably because of everything I just mentioned. The Holy Spirit absolutely, *completely* healed my heart, filled me with peace, and made me new. I don't have any guilt, shame, or pent-up anger over the things I experienced as a child. He took it all. I will always grieve the loss of my niece and feel the sadness related to her death, but I have peace knowing her life mattered and she is strongly loved and remembered. My spirit is free from these things. But genetically I do have a predisposition to several forms of mental illness.

I saw an illustration online that helped explain it to me. Imagine that we start off as a cup, and the cup represents our ability to cope. Certain circumstances and experiences add a little more water to our cup. Genetics and family history add a little. Drug use, financial stress, pressure, overwhelm, tragedy, traumatic experiences, relationship struggles, and more—all continue to add more water to your cup. When your cup can hold no more and begins to overflow, that is when mental illness may show itself. For me personally, it's a pileup of pressure and expectations.

Some people like to sit at the edge of the ocean because they like the way it feels when the water pulls the sand out from under their legs. That's the way I feel when I'm overwhelmed with responsibilities. Like every new thing that has to be taken care of, every new request, every add-on to an already full tray of plates is sucking the sand out from under me and I'm sinking deeper and deeper. I can feel the pull of everyone's wants and needs, and before I know it, I'm drowning. I'm stuck in the undertow. I can't breathe, I can't stop spinning, and I don't know which direction to face to swim for the surface. That's when I begin biting my fingers off, sprinting out of the kitchen to escape the sounds of my children playing, snapping at everyone around me, shutting myself off, curling up in bed unable to move for a week, and binge-eating everything in my kitchen, followed by self-loathing and an empty kind of sadness.

I stopped laughing as much behind the scenes. For a season I became the girl in the videos cracking everyone up with my torn-up thumbs, struggling in silence to pinpoint what was going on with my joy. I had to have that breakdown in Cheddars. I had to let it all out, admit I was struggling, and seek help. Just talking openly about it helped so much. Maybe that was part of God's command for me to "speak" all those years ago. I'm getting the help I need. I'm doing much better just by being open about my experience. I'm getting blood tests to check on my hormones and thyroid and make sure everything is okay. In the meantime, I've done a lot of research on coping mechanisms and continue to be open about what I have experienced.

> Give all your worries and cares to God, for he cares about you. (1 Peter 5:7)

I haven't had a deeply depressed spell in a while, and for that I'm extremely thankful. But anxiety has continued to be fairly regular. I know many people associate anxiety with fear, but when I feel anxiety triggered by stress, I handle it. I cope. I push through it until I can breathe again. Anxiety physically happens out of nowhere as a response to my surroundings. Fear is often hypothetical, associated with what-ifs. I have anxiety sometimes, *and* I still laugh without fear. I don't dwell on worried thoughts or allow my imagination to control my actions, because I know who I belong to. When I'm physically anxious, I am not afraid because I know it will pass.

> Then you will experience God's peace, which exceeds anything we can understand. His peace will guard your hearts and minds as you live in Christ Jesus. (Philippians 4:7)

Now, I also want to be honest about something else. It is absolutely possible to be completely healed of your struggles, both mental and physical. I do believe in the healing and restoring work of the Holy Spirit. So many have been completely set free from their struggles with mental health, and I don't want to seem like I don't believe that happens. I just want to help people understand that even Christians suffer, and if a person isn't experiencing the healing miracle that others have, it isn't automatically because they just don't love Jesus enough or have enough faith. Treating people this way has led to so many believers struggling in silence for fear of judgment and shame. That's why it's so important that in the middle of whatever obstacle you are facing, you *listen* to Him. Nobody else.

When I'm feeling the most out of control, stressed out, down, and anxious, I have to admit that I'm usually more wrapped up in people than in God and His Word. Time spent with Him in prayer and silence goes hand in hand with peace that will help you find clarity on what you need to do. Cast your cares on the Lord, then listen and trust His guidance. What He guides your spirit to do matters more than what anyone thinks of you. I'm at peace with what I've learned in the struggle of mental health, faith, and fear. I do not feel ashamed or to blame for depression or anxiety any more than I'd feel like my stubbed toe was because I took my eyes off Jesus. God has proven to me over and over that there is no struggle I face in vain. I was griping away in prayer one day about how embarrassing it is to be a Christian with a platform coming off such an incredible year of testament to faith, then suddenly struggling to feel peace. God interrupted my whining to remind me of my favorite scripture, Romans 8:28. God works for the good in all things for those who love Him and have been called according to His purpose. Sometimes I don't like the things I go through, no matter how much value can be passed on as a result of them. But at the end of it all, I know the greatest commandment is to love God and love others. Going through things and sharing what we learn is a way to love others.

First Thessalonians 5:18 says to "be thankful in all circumstances." Give thanks through the seasons of joy, peace, and progress. Give thanks in seasons of grief, confusion, and setbacks. The hardest times in your life set you up for the deepest impact. I try to remain faithful in the hard times, trusting that God has a purpose for whatever I'm going through. It doesn't feel good, but the things that feel the worst create a deeper appreciation for the bliss that follows. If you've been feeling like you've lost yourself, you are not alone. God hasn't forgotten you, abandoned you, or gotten mad at you. You aren't supposed to have it all together all the time. Our flesh isn't always in line with the truth, but there is nothing we go through that can't be used as long as we listen when He shows us the way.

What has the whispering voice been urging you to do? Have you felt a tug in a certain direction but have fought acknowledging it because you're afraid it isn't the right path? Choosing fear over faith only prolongs the time you spend in a state of stress and confusion. I promise once you listen, you will realize God is leading you exactly where you need to be. It's kind of like your first day on a new job. You feel really nervous because it's a brand-new place filled with new people, and you have a lot to learn. Goodness, I'll never forget my first day as a waitress when I had to learn to take an order, push the right buttons, keep from spitting when I talk-ed, and serve those dang flimsy glasses of wine without spilling them. I actually did end up spilling and break-ing an entire tray of wine. *Onto* a group of women. Who didn't laugh even a little bit. But by the end of the first week, I was laughing out a sigh of relief while multitasking like you've never seen. I like to think that job prepared me for motherhood. Cleaning up messes I didn't make without being thanked, bringing a person exactly what they asked for but now don't want, and standing in the kitchen scarfing down some bread before someone caught me were all excellent preparation, so I'm thankful I went in that direction.

When the Lord is tugging at you, deep down you know it. Maybe it's a change of location, a new job, a decision to pursue or leave a relationship, or a change of lifestyle. Whatever it may be, I want you to know you don't have to be afraid. Even if you spill a whole tray of wine your first day on the job, you've been led where you are for a reason. A woman who chooses to listen can laugh through decisions that are tough. The direction God leads you may feel scary, but following His guidance means choosing faith and trust.

She laughs while she listens in seasons of doubt, knowing His guidance will help her figure it out.

Chapter 7

—888—

She Breaks

When all the people of Israel saw the fire coming
down and the glorious presence of the LORD filling
the Temple, they fell face down on the ground and
worshiped and praised the LORD, saying, "He is
good! His faithful love endures forever!"
2 CHRONICLES 7:3

It was one of those weeks. The kind where each day
you're having to talk yourself through it. I was barely
making it. My brain had just about reached its capa-
city and could hardly process a single thing more.

Well. . .in our living room there is a good spot. Do
y'all have a "good spot" in your home? It's the best place
to sit in the house. It's the most comfortable, has the
best back support, is optimally positioned for TV view-
ing, and the only person who sits in it 99 percent of
the time is my husband. He has pretty much claimed
it. To the point that if I'm sitting in it, I can feel his
annoyance as he reluctantly sits in the other chair. It's
one of those stupid things that causes married people
to get really mad at each other.

On this day that shall forever be known as "the day

I scared my husband," it had been a week since I'd even had a chance to just sit and relax. I finally had a moment, and my husband was downstairs playing music. I was so relieved that I could just sit for a minute, in the good spot, and catch up on a show. Aahhhh, to finally just relax and let my brain chill out for a while. I kid you not, less than two minutes after I sat down, I heard him coming up the stairs, almost as if he knew someone had sat down in "his" spot. Just like the kids when you get on the phone or open up a bag of chips to sit in the bathtub and eat in peace.

When he stepped into the room and just stood there, I decided not to even turn my head because today was not the day and I was not the one. I was trying so hard to tap into the Jesus in me and keep my peace, and I just knew this was a test. So I went on watching my show, determined not to engage even though his presence hovering over me already had my blood getting hot, because this is a public community spot! He sighed one of those sighs that you can easily blame on just catching your breath, but I knew better. I'm the queen of sighs, and it was an "I can't believe she's not getting up, knowing that's my spot" sigh. I pursed my lips, refusing to participate in any kind of argument. He turned and walked away, and I sang to myself, "Oh victory in Jesus"—until I heard him go into our bedroom.

I have a weird thing about my bed. It's almost an OCD need for the blankets to be neat. No corners turned up or uneven. I wish I was like this about the neatness of my whole house, but it's just my bed. My husband knows this. He is the destroyer of beds. One of those sleepers who somehow pushes the sheet all the way down to the foot of the bed and has half the top blanket twisted upside down and the other half on the floor. I, on the other hand, wake up with the sheet and blankets still perfectly in place as if no one has even been there. A few times I've actually fixed the sheet and blankets with him still in the bed in the middle of the night because it bothers me so much. He doesn't sleep in the bed much, because he's a night owl. So the bed is kind of "my spot." He rarely spends much time in our bedroom, so as soon as he went in there, I knew it was just to get under my skin, because. . .marriage, right? But I stayed put and just kept trying to choose joy. He walked out of the bedroom and went into the bathroom. I heard the drawer open and the clinky sound of the nail clippers. But after he retrieved the clippers, I heard him walk back into the bedroom. Then I heard the creak of him sitting on the bed.

My blood started to get warm in anticipation of the incredibly stupid thing he was about to do for no other reason than to get back at me for being in his spot. . .in the *living room*, which is community space! It happened. He did it. I heard it. *Clink. . .clink. . .* My shoulders started bouncing with every clip. I couldn't take it. Like a mature adult does, I got up and calmly stomped my feet as hard as I could down the hall to politely let him know it worked. He had gotten me up, and I was coming to have a chat about it. I gently kicked in the door like warrior princesses do and walked in to see him doing exactly what I knew he was doing. Sitting in the middle of my destroyed bedsheets clipping his toenails.

I looked at him and said, "What do you think you're doing?"—even though I knew he knew I knew exactly what he was doing. He looked up at me and smugly said, "Nothin'," as he snipped *another* toenail there in my bed right in front of my face. Then he did it, y'all. He took his hand and swiped all the toenail clippings up in the air. In slow motion, I saw them float down all over my sheets. And that's the moment my spirit left my body and took all the chill in me with it. My soul went over to watch the show with the Lord and talk about all the things we were gonna have to talk about after this.

I said, "Okay. Okay. That's how you wanna be? Okay. I can be petty. Did you forget where I come from?" Have you ever noticed when people get really mad, wherever they are from is the toughest place on earth? Like "I'm from the suburbs of Peaceville County, okay, you don't even know!" Except I really did grow up kind of rough in a pretty scary trailer park that one did not simply go for a walk in. So I went back to my hillbilly roots and said, "Did you forget I'm from the country? I'm about to go redneck woman all over you. I'm about to show you crazy." Then I slung my head forward and told him, "I am *tipped* over. You have done *tipped* me over. I'm a little psychopot from the South; tip me over and my crazy comes out."

Have you ever gotten so mad at your spouse you made up an angry lullaby and sang it at him? I thought it was actually kind of impressive. Then I hopped out of the room fueled by toenail fury and went on a mission to destroy as many of his things as possible. What does he enjoy, what does he like, what can I mess up? Dr Pepper. He needs DP in the house at all times. So I went to the kitchen, gathered his DP cans, went to the front door, and *whoosh*—slung 'em into the yard. But it had been snowing, so really they were just gonna be extra cold when he brought them back in, so that wasn't good enough. I stomped downstairs loud enough for him to know I was heading downstairs where all his guitars were. All three of our girls were playing down there, so I flew around the corner and calmly said, "Oh, hey, girls, y'all just keep playing. Nothing to see here." About that time, he poked his head down the stairs looking worried and carefully asked, "What are you doing?" So while I tried unsuccessfully to type in the code on the guitar safe, I replied the same way he did upstairs. "Nothin'. Good thing you changed the code."

Truthfully, I'm glad I couldn't get into the safe because I wasn't about to actually do anything to his guitars, and it would have ruined my crazy lady vibe if I'd opened it and done nothing. So I proceeded to aggressively take all his music posters off the wall, but then gently set them down because I actually like them too. But at least he was gonna have to put them all back. I flew back up the stairs, went in the bathroom, grabbed his toothbrush, and slung it across the living room. He shut the basement door in time to see his toothbrush fly by. "Was that my toothbrush? Seriously?" At this point he followed me back into the bedroom like a terrified lost puppy, and as every one of his T-shirts flew over his head, he pleaded, "Babe, hey, babe, I'm sorry. Can you just calm down, please? I didn't mean to make you so upset." To which I replied, "That's exactly what you meant to do. This is what you wanted. This is what you get."

He said he was gonna take the girls to get ice cream and give me some space. To which I threw a shirt at his head and said, "Oh, I'm clearing out all kinds of space." Then they left, and I came back to myself and fell to the floor. Heart racing, sweating, and barely able to breathe, I started sobbing. I texted my sister, "I just threw everything my husband owns into the hallway." She responded, "Why? What did he do?" To which I had to reply, "He clipped his toenails in my bed." I stared at the sentence I had just typed out and went from crying uncontrollably to laughing hysterically. Crying and laughing go hand in hand, don't they? Laughter is sometimes the only thing that can pull you out of your crazy and lift your spirits back to reality. It is *such* a gift.

I laugh about that story now, and it's one of my favorite stories to tell, because in so many ways it really was hilarious, but also because I know I'm not the only one who has had a come-apart on the ones I love the most. I do exaggerate a bit of it for humor, but for the most part that's exactly what happened. I realized that day that I needed help. Not loony-bin help, but help in life. I needed to communicate to my husband that he would have to take on more responsibility before I ended up in the hospital from a stress-induced heart attack. I also realized I couldn't run from anxiety anymore. I'd been telling myself I was fine for way too long. I wasn't fine. Suddenly feeling like I may black out at the grocery store or around a bunch of people, uncontrollably chewing my fingers to shreds, and wanting to curl into a ball when there are too many loud sounds in a small space aren't just part of my personality; they are anxiety. These idiosyncrasies have always been there, but in the past year they've become worse and worse as I've gotten more and more overwhelmed as well as hormonal. Womanhood is fun, isn't it?

> *Don't worry about anything; instead, pray about everything. Tell God what you need, and thank him for all he has done. Then you will experience God's peace, which exceeds anything we can understand. His peace will guard your hearts and minds as you live in Christ Jesus.* (Philippians 4:6–7)

Knowing that Bible verse used to make me anxious

about feeling anxious, you know what I mean? It had me feeling like I'd failed at having strong faith. I love the Lord so much and know that His plans for me are good. I truly don't doubt that I am loved. Anxiety, in my case, isn't rooted in some deep fear of people, places, or an unknown future. It's rooted more in pleasing others. I get physically ill at the thought of disappointing people, cracking under pressure, failing to meet expectations, and falling short of serving my calling to its fullest extent. As I dive deeper into pursuing God's purpose for me, more distractions begin to pop up from all angles. Requests and opportunities that didn't come from God but from people. It's easy for me to mix up my faith that I can do all things through Christ with shouldering too many things that He didn't give me. Next thing I know, I've taken on too much and feel like giving up. This is a struggle I kept to myself for a while because of a fear of judgment from others. I'm sure y'all can relate to the aggravation of someone picking apart your faith, which is so near and dear to your heart. Here's the thing: regardless of the assumptions anyone else makes about your closeness to God, your relationship with Him and your struggles are known best by *Him*. He knows your heart. He knows your ups and downs. He understands where you're coming from. He has already prepared the lessons for you to learn through it all. No person's opinion changes any of that. So be more afraid of listening to them over Him than of what they may think. God will knock you over the head with conviction and realization when the time is right and you are ready. I'll tell you mine, even though it's hard to admit it. As I say yes to more than I should, my time spent with Him is replaced with ways to cope with stress. So silly since He is the best stress reliever. He gets put on the back burner while I eat, sleep, pace around, and drown Him out with reality TV. That's what I do when I've taken on too much. I try to avoid my responsibilities, which only contributes to my anxiety. I was so afraid of people questioning my faith, because deep down I knew I wasn't putting God first anymore, and that hurt.

I share this with y'all because I want you to know you aren't the only one breaking down sometimes. It doesn't make you weak, crazy, or a bad person. It makes you human. Take a deep breath and remember how important it is to set boundaries and say no sometimes. It took a complete breakdown for me to realize without a doubt that I can't do it all. I can't take care of my kids, take care of my home, be a supportive wife, be a good friend, stay successful in my career, serve God's calling on my life, care for my own self, and keep my bedsheets symmetrical on my own. I need simple, and I need discernment. I can't be everything to everybody. I need to be okay with disappointing someone if what they ask of me isn't in alignment with where God wants my focus. It's hard to feel joy when you're consumed with worry.

The more things you say yes to, the more you have to worry about. You have limits. Yes, you can do all things in Christ who strengthens you. All the things He has called you to. Not all the things people pile onto your shoulders. If your time and relationship with Him begin to suffer, you know it's time to step back and do some trimming.

Breakdowns are a sure sign that you are in need of some time with Jesus. I once found myself crying in the bathroom because I was stuck in my cute strappy sports bra. Can't even try to take care of myself without being personally attacked by my undergarments. I burn more calories fiddling with my sports bra than I do during the actual workout. I figured since it was almost July, I might need to start working on my summer body. But y'all, I got so upset trying to put my sports bra *on* that I threw an actual fit. I wasn't even sweaty yet. Alone on my bathroom floor, naked from my high-waisted yoga pants up, except for the twisted-up sports bra stuck under my armpits. Arms flailing around, huffing and puffing, grunting, pacing back and forth. I almost dislocated my shoulder trying to squeeze my fingers far enough underneath the back of those super-stylish, way-too-expensive, crisscross Kiva straps from the Facebook ad. I felt like I was trying to escape from some sinister kidnapper's undergarment shackles. If the key to freedom was the removal of my sports bra, I'd never be seen again.

Twenty minutes later, and I was sitting on the bathroom floor sweating, failing at life, and feeling completely defeated. Conquered by my underwears, y'all. All I wanted to do was maybe work out, and now I was tired just from *dressing* for it. I started crying because I couldn't believe I was about to have to cut my bra off my body with scissors. Is this what a midthirties mom life crisis looks like? I want my twenties back, when I reached down and whipped my bra over my head with ease and my prebirth chesticles didn't get caught in the straps or bounce off my face. I didn't have any use for a tata towel. (That's a towel made specifically for the absorption of underboob sweat because your tig ol' bitties take a nap on your stomach when you sit.) Take me back to the days before dressing for the workout _was_ the workout.

I caught my pitiful reflection in the mirror. Sitting there defeated, hunched over on the floor, arms turning purple, feeling light-headed, I thought, _You are not gonna die like this._ I put on a motivational speech with a perfect mix of classical music and Arnold Schwarzenegger quotes, rubbed my QVC easy-pay Josie Maran argan oil all over my skin, did some jumping jacks to help my arms wake up, peed myself a little from the jumping jacks, did somewhere between zero and one push-ups on my knees, chugged an energy drink. . .and it happened. I popped my shoulder blade out of place, cracked a rib, folded my body in half, and slid that sports bra right off. Tears of sweet relief overwhelmed my soul. I stared at that bra like, _Never again, evil one._ And _that_, my friends, is why I can't work out. It's just not worth the sports bra tizzy fit. When you feel yourself exaggerating on this level, it may be a sign you need a break. But it really is so frustrating not having the upper-body strength to get that thing over your head. I never expected to feel so emotional over something so silly like I was that day, but a good breakdown is usually triggered by something unexpected.

Something unexpected actually happened today, and it broke my heart. The sun was shining. The sky was blue. My best friend called to see if I needed a break from writing and wanted to bring my girls to swim with her girls. My first instinct was to say no. I had so much work left to do. But her bestie intuition was right, because I desperately needed some fresh air to clear up some space for creativity to flow. So I gathered my girls, who were ecstatic to go, and we were gonna have a nice day. We were sitting on the deck doing our mom thing. Somewhat catching up, but mostly keeping track of our seven kids. All of a sudden a school bus passed by. We heard her dog bark, followed by a thud, and then the bus drove off. We looked at each other, hoping that sound wasn't what we thought it was. She went out front while I watched the kids. I held her toddler, terrified of what I had a feeling she was about to find. Then I heard it. The sounds of my best friend finding her dog lifeless in the front yard. I could feel her sorrow in my chest just from the sounds of her cries. She'd just lost a member of their family that she'd taken care of, cuddled, and loved for eight years. I told her to go into the bedroom and let it all out as long as she needed to while I took care of the kids, because something I've learned about intense, unexpected grief is that the only way to gather yourself, breathe, and move forward is to feel what you're feeling.

Anger, guilt, sorrow, regret. It's okay to feel them. You need to feel them so you can cry them out and let them go every single time they hit you. Tears wash away the pent-up emotions that are blocking your creativity, preventing your healing, and prolonging your pain. In the moments after an emotional release, you can find so much clarity.

> The LORD is close to the brokenhearted and saves those who are crushed in spirit.
> (Psalm 34:18 NIV)

So go ahead and let yourself break. Whatever the reason may be. When the stresses of life have clouded up all the space in your heart, a breakdown brings you closer to the One who will give you back your spark. The One who will give you back your ability to laugh.

I've noticed that the stronger I try to be, the farther I stray from my connection to Christ. We cannot run from the feelings that hurt us while staying near the love that conquers them all. Finding yourself defeated might mean you need an emotional release. I know what it's like to feel like you need to keep it all together. When my niece was battling cancer at Saint Jude, I stayed strong during my visit. I smiled while we played Connect Four, held back tears while I tickled her palms, and kept fear off my face in the middle of helping her breathe while they cleaned her trache. I swallowed groans of sorrow at her bedside late at night. Sat in silence staring at her tiny, fragile, six-year-old body stuffed with tubes so my sister could get a little sleep. I didn't feel God's presence in the midst of my determination to keep it together. But when I got home, sitting in the car in my garage all alone, I completely broke. It was there, in the depths of my sorrow, that He saved me. He was always near me, but I couldn't feel it or see it until I let go.

How many times have you powered through a day telling yourself everything's okay? Release it to Him. Don't put off the fall. Go ahead and fall apart. Curl into a ball on the floor. Acknowledge your grief and let yourself be weak. Cry away. Cry until you can laugh again, because you *can*. Because there's nothing wrong with needing to cry. Keeping the pain inside doesn't make what's hurting you go away. It just prevents you from accepting change. When unexpected things happen, everything changes. That's scary for many of us. As the saying goes, "Nothing changes if nothing changes."

Often though, change is positive. When Christ comes into your life, you can expect some major changes. Christ changes your heart, your desires, your perspective, and the possibilities of your future. Plan to stay on your toes, because only heaven knows the power of your purpose. Every single thing, *every single thing*, that you experience in your life has power to impact others. Especially the moments that make you cry.

I don't know what makes you think you need to hold it all in. Grief, sorrow, and every other overwhelming emotion are just part of being human. Jesus cried out in several different scriptures in the Bible. The shortest verse in God's word is John 11:35: "Jesus wept." There is so much significance to the power and necessity of weeping in this verse. Jesus had traveled to Bethany to raise Lazarus from the dead. After speaking to Lazarus's sisters, Martha and Mary, He wept. Why do you think Jesus wept even though He was just moments away from awakening Lazarus from death?

Compassion.

Jesus Christ is the embodiment of love, and love is deeply compassionate. Have you ever seen someone you care for struggling through something and felt your heart break for them? It's almost impossible not to shed tears when those you care for are hurting. Jesus felt the pain of Lazarus's loved ones. Even knowing that death is not final, He wept for the sorrow felt in the wake of their loss. It's okay for you to grieve your losses. It's okay for you to weep, break down, or even break things out of anger. It's okay to be a believer, knowing death has been conquered, and still feel the emotions that tie love and loss together. Jesus knows what you're feeling. He feels it with you. Jesus wept over the damage left by death and the wages of sin. He weeps for every loss you feel, every tragedy, every sickness, and every sin of every person in this world. Thank God, He gave us laughter.

Have you ever been so upset that you found yourself laughing uncontrollably? When my heart is exposed, for some reason so is my funny bone. It reminds me of a scene in the movie *Steel Magnolias*. If you haven't seen this movie, first of all, you're welcome for exposing you to it; and second, where in the world have you been? It's probably one of the greatest tearjerkers of all time, but also absolutely hilarious. Spoiler ahead, and I don't feel bad about it because you're about thirty years late. Right after burying her young daughter, a mother finally allows herself to be overwhelmed with grief. As Sally Field gives a spot-on performance of absolute devastation, everyone watching is crying their eyes out. Her character, M'Lynn, goes from crying out in sorrow, to walking back and forth determined to make sense of it, to screaming in desperate anger, "I just wanna hit something. I wanna hit it hard!" And at that moment as all her friends look on helplessly, her sarcastically hilarious friend, Clairee, steps forward, grabbing the arm of the group grouch, Ouiser (Weezer), and shouts, "Here! Hit this! Slap her. We'll sell T-shirts that say 'I slapped Ouiser Boudreaux.'" Caught off guard, the group stands in shock as she continues, "M'Lynn, you just missed the chance of a lifetime. Half the people in Chinquapin Parish would give their eye teeth to take a whack at Ouiser!" M'Lynn and the group erupt in uncontrollable laughter. Tense times desperately need a moment of laughter. To go from crying to cry laughing is a wonderful gift of emotional release. Grief can lock you up in the dark if you hang out there too long. Comic relief helps you see the light again.

Don't ever be afraid to encounter circumstances in life that might make you cry. Tear-stained cheeks tell life-changing stories. Whether they are tears of sorrow or joy, the power of emotion is the way it strengthens our connection with others.

She laughs in the face of tears, knowing God works

for the good in all of her fears.

Thank goodness we have access to a never-ending Supplier of love, joy, and peace. Yeah, we can handle our stress with booze, food, and toddler-tantrum fits. But the drinks run dry, the wintergreen Tums get expensive, and your enraged stool smash only satisfies for five. . .okay, twenty seconds.

Second Chronicles 7:3 (NIV) says, "When all the Israelites *saw*. . .the glory of the LORD. . ." Have you been too distracted to see it? Sometimes the reason behind our season of struggle is that we need to be humbled enough to see Him. When the enemy has stripped me of my sanity, God shows up and shows out for me. That's what's so jump-up-and-down exhilarating about being a child of God. Every scheme of the enemy only brings us that much closer to realizing who we belong to. When He breaks us, God can finally be the strength in our weakness. Oddly enough, when we're broken, our knees hit the pavement and our faces rest on the ground where His voice is the only sound. His peace never runs out. He is good. His love endures forever.

Breakdowns remind you a break is in order. Life is full of crazy days. If we can't laugh, we'll forever feel anxious about what tomorrow may bring instead of brimming with excitement for the good things in store each day. Somehow we get it stuck in our heads that a strong woman of God isn't supposed to break. She isn't supposed to freak out and yell or let herself cry. She's supposed to keep it all together all the time. But honey, what makes a woman strong in faith is knowing the God she serves does His best work on those He can mold. When you allow yourself to break, you give Him room to create a new gift in you. We need to lean into His strength, but when we try to keep it all together, we tend to box Him out. Appreciate your moments of weakness. It is in those moments we get a front row seat to the power of Jesus. The Carpenter creates beautiful woodwork from broken branches. Don't be afraid to fall. Don't be afraid to make mistakes.

She laughs, knowing when she's had all she can take, He lifts her up when *she breaks*.

Chapter 8

***

She Forgives

"When you are praying, first forgive anyone you are holding a grudge against, so that your Father in heaven will forgive your sins, too."

MARK 11:25

Now y'all know there's gotta be mention of forgiveness if you want to have freedom in your spirit to laugh without fear. Don't you dare skip this chapter just because you aren't ready to stop being mad! If I can forgive my husband for driving right past the drop-off at the hospital and parking the car in the hospital parking lot when I was 6 centimeters dilated and crawling up the ceiling of the car in pain, you can let go of some stuff too. Did you know women in labor can crawl straight up walls like Spider-Man? Oh yes. I'm pretty sure that's why my husband was so terrified of me by the time we left the house. He had the audacity to ask if I was sure it was labor. So after I speed-crawled up the wall to the ceiling and over to where he was standing, smacked him on the back of the head, and jumped off the wall with a back flip, he got in the car. We can also speed-wobble across a parking lot while cussing out our husband so fast the world around us moves in slow motion. To make it worse, when I made it inside, they handed me some papers to fill out in the waiting room. I couldn't even remember my own name by that point, much less how to hold a pen. This was five years ago, and I've clearly moved on. I never bring it up to my husband when I'm mad or anything.

People always say, "I can forgive, but I won't forget." I do think it's important to learn from the actions of others and set boundaries to maintain healthy relationships over toxic ones. But I think a lot of people can't move on from their anger or shame because they dwell on what someone has done to them. I still have days now and then when I have flashes of how I felt when I was molested by my cousin. Images of her locking the door to "play house" with me pop into my brain out of nowhere right in the middle of a great day. These used to be the thoughts I shoved down any way I could. I'd bury my feelings under drugs, drinking, clubs, and bad relationships. I'd toss as many self-destructing distractions over my dirty memory as I could. Hide my skeletons under *other* things that made me feel guilty. I kept telling myself I was over it and didn't even care anymore, while staring at my face falling off in a mirror after taking a drop of acid. I felt hopeless, alone, and ashamed of myself through most of my high school days, and I carried this hidden guilt with me most of my life. I know it's what hindered me from truly feeling peace and purpose for so long.

I didn't forgive my dad until the day I gave all my chains to God. The worst thing he even did was doing nothing. For a long time, even I couldn't tell you why he was such a sore spot for me. Until the day God set me free. I knew it was because I loved him so much. I needed him. I needed a father. I longed for stability, security, and acknowledgment. As a little girl, despite how hard my mom tried, she couldn't give me what I needed from my dad. I couldn't understand why he didn't care how much we were struggling or why he didn't want to help take care of us. As I grew older, the longing I had for his presence turned into resentment. So when he started wanting to spend time with us, I felt annoyed instead of glad. He'd have us come over, and he'd clearly be really happy to see us. He would cook for us and beg us to stay the night. He's such a kind-spirited goofball, and I see so much of myself in him—which almost made me feel more irritated. I just couldn't let go of the trouble that his absence in our childhood caused our family. As a result, I'd be really cold toward him and say hurtful things—things that were true but I knew would hurt his feelings. Then I started to do what a lot of us do. I started to make my own bad decisions and blame him for them. I used my daddy issues as an excuse to be reckless.

I don't know why we cling to our pain the way we do. It's like feeling bad feels good. That's why there are so many hateful people running around just looking for someone to unleash the beast on. An angry outburst is so satisfying to someone carrying a bottomless pit of resentment. Letting go feels so much better than being stuck. Have you ever burned out your shoulders by holding your arms up for too long? Maybe while carrying the most precious balloon of your child's life around the carnival all night, or trying to break the world hula hoop record, or endlessly blow-drying your super-thick hair. Finally putting your arm down is such a relief.

One time my shoulders were absolutely on fire when my arms got stuck trying to put on a romper. I have this weird addiction to rompers. I have a fancy romper for rompin' at the Olive Garden, a casual romper for laid-back rompin' at the Walmarts, and even a camo country romper (also known as overalls) for blending in while looking cute. Either it's because I know I'm not having any more babies and wanna dress myself like one, or it's because my husband doesn't like them. Either way, I can't manage to walk past one without wanting to try it on.

I was at a cute little local boutique looking for something fancy, like a graphic tee without any holes in it. From across the store glimmered a sequined golden romper. It drew me in like a mosquito to skin when it's nighttime and humid. The next thing I knew, I was in full-out panic mode, stuck in a romper inside the dressing room of the local boutique. First of all, it wasn't my size, and I knew it. But I wanted to make it fit, girl. So I squeezed my butt through the waist hole and managed to get one arm all the way in. The problem is, shorts rompers aren't ideal if you're tall. So although I got my one arm in, I couldn't stand up straight without giving myself an atomic wedgie. This was the moment I realized the golden sparkle romper was a mistake. But I was in too deep, so I thought I'd try to get my other hand in and just see. I was bent halfway over with my other arm through the sleeve to my elbow, and I couldn't move. I panicked. I started sweating and trying not to cry while thrashing around, trying to break my hand free, looking like a crazy lady trying to escape her straitjacket. I was so scared I was gonna have to poke my head through the dressing room curtain door and ask for help like, "Ma'am, I think this one's gonna have to come home with me unless you can help me get it off." That was the day I realized I'm not meant for fancy shiny golden shorts rompers. I knew better, but sometimes we have to learn the hard, embarrassing, hilarious way. She laughs without fear of rompers now that she once got stuck in one in public.

The anger of unforgiveness is like that deceivingly pretty romper. You think you deserve it, but once you try it on, it's really hard to get it off. Next thing you know you're stuck, traumatized, and feeling a little bad about yourself. See how a little humor helps make tough messages easier to swallow? Next time you feel angry thinking about someone who riles you up, just imagine me in my romper with half my body tangled up. Being unable to take off the hurt you've been wearing will burn you out. The sweet relief of the weight released when you let go of that pain you carry will free you up to truly heal and enjoy your future to the fullest.

Challenge someone to forgive the person who hurt them the most and watch how defensive they get. When

I tell my mama to forgive Dad, I gotta duck and dodge the daggers in her stare. She'll say, "I forgave that man a long time ago." But I don't think you can get all riled up and ruffled feathers at the mention of a person you've truly forgiven. Baby steps, Mama. Don't get mad at me. . .I love you.

It almost seems like we don't want the peace we know deep down we will get from forgiveness.

When you receive the gifts and fruit of the Spirit, you begin to have an understanding wash over you about things that have hurt you deeply. The gift of wisdom helps you to see past your own emotions so you can be humble enough to acknowledge that not everything is about you. In my own personal situation, I had to recognize that the pain I felt and the struggle we faced were real. The role my dad played in our hardships was real. But it never occurred to me that he was a broken human being too, and he couldn't give us what he didn't have. I was much older when I felt a tug to learn more about who my dad was and the factors that shaped the decisions he made. So I asked my mom, and what she told me broke my heart.

My dad was beaten and abused as a child by his stepdad. His real dad had no interest in having a relationship with him or us. I remember meeting him one time when I was really little, and he barely looked at us. My dad is a talented musician, a very gifted drummer. He was even offered a scholarship to join the band at the University of Alabama. But he chose being in a rock band instead to pursue making it big in music. He's an alcoholic. Has been since before my mom met him. You know how you can smell something, and it takes you right to a memory, a place, or a person? For example, Black & Mild cigars in the air take me straight to my papa sitting in his recliner holding the wooden end piece between his dentures. Well, the smell of Budweiser was the cologne of my dad. No matter where he was or what he was doing, you can bet there was a beer in his hand and a cooler nearby for the next one. When I look at him now (once every year or so), I see a man full of regret. He has so many endearing qualities. Handsome, super goofy, fun to be around, hopelessly trusting, loves having friends around and cooking for everyone, laughs nonstop at his own jokes, and is musically gifted in a way that I've always felt proud of. I see him as a person who went through a lot of hard things as a child and didn't respond well. He allowed his own lack of forgiveness to fuel bad decisions for which he never took responsibility. At some point it dawned on me. . .I did the same.

I made a ton of bad decisions and put myself in dangerous positions that I justified in my mind because of things I'd gone through. If I had the addictive personality or dependency in my own genes, I easily could have gone down the same path. It's a vicious cycle of bad decisions due to a lack of forgiveness. I no longer look at my dad as an absent parent who didn't care about us. I no longer blame him for everything that went wrong in my own childhood.

God helped me to understand that the people in our lives are more than just what we want them to be. They carry their own hurts, traumas, and problems. So my dad's inability to be the father I wanted wasn't because I wasn't good enough or loved. It was because he didn't know how to overcome his own demons. I am continually working on completely forgiving my dad. I don't have it in me to pursue a relationship, but that's not what forgiveness means. You can replace hard feelings with well wishes for someone while continuing to protect your own peace. The phone call I'd avoided for years went pretty much like this: *Hey, Dad, just wanted to say hi and see how you've been. . . . That's good. Well, I can't talk long. I just wanted to let you know I do love you. I have had hard feelings for a long time, but I forgive you and hope you're doing well. . . . I know. I know, Dad. . . . Okay. I gotta go. . . . Okay. Talk to you soon. . . . Love you too. . . . Okay. Bye.* I set myself free by letting him know that I do love him and forgive him. I wish he could have made better decisions, and I pray he finds peace. I cry every time I see him because he is my dad, and I see so much of me in him. I feel compassion in my heart for him, and I know it comes from the love of Jesus within me.

Deep down you know what you need to do. When someone's words really blow your mind, hit you right in the heart, and stir up your spirit, it's usually because you already knew what was said. You just needed it brought to the surface.

We tend to fight acknowledging that there is a better perspective of what forgiveness means in your life no matter what it is you're holding onto. I think you know right this moment what is holding you back. You know who you need to forgive. You know you need to quit fighting it. You know your soul is desperate to be released from the residual negativity built up by your refusal to truly let go of anger and bitterness. You know forgiveness doesn't justify pain, and you know holding on to the past steals joy from your future. If you want to be filled with the Spirit of Christ and all the peace that comes with it, you've got to give up your resentment. You are made new once you lay it all down, and that means you're free from identifying with anything anyone has put you through.

It's so easy to say we have forgiven someone, so much easier than truly letting go. Some losses cut us so deep, they almost take us with them. Have you ever been hurt so badly you didn't think you'd ever smile much less laugh again?

My best friend lost her older brother when he committed suicide. He was only twenty-four years old. I asked her if she had forgiven him. She quickly said yes. But then she sent me an open letter she'd written to him revealing how she truly felt:

> *I was asked to talk about forgiveness when it comes to your suicide.*
> *Forgiveness is a strong word.*
> *A word I dabble in. But realize now I am not yet ready to commit.*
> *I love you forever and always.*
> *Nothing will ever, EVER change that fact.*
> *But you did something, not only to me,*

but to our whole family that makes
    forgiveness complex.
I am not who I was before the day you made
    your great escape.
I self-medicate and self-destruct.
I have wanted to feel as low as you must
    have felt.
Because of the guilt of not knowing
    you felt that low.

I sit here eleven years later and find myself
    stuck on forgiveness and suicide.
A subject that was supposedly going to
    become my new normal yet has
    not delivered.
It's not normal that you aren't here.
It's not normal that you took your own life.
It's not normal that our parents found you
    that way.
And it's not normal that my dad cannot
    speak of it.

You left this world.
You left us.

You left people who would've helped
you in a second.
But we're supposed to know that it wasn't
our fault.
We're supposed to know there's nothing we
could've done.
We're supposed to understand what we'll
never understand.
I am mad.
And I love you.
And I guess I'm saying feeling both will
have to do.
I accept the unknowns.
And I do that because I love you.
That is the beat of my forgiving drum.

Forgetting?
That's the hard part.

I don't forget our childhood.
I don't forget our conversations.
I don't forget the hints I must have missed that
plague me with the worst grotesque guilt.
I don't forget the years of torture to my mind.

I don't forget the part where you never
    mentioned what you're going through.
I don't forget you were my best friend.
I don't forget you waited up for me until I drove
    home from college in crazy stormy weather.
I don't forget that you always had my back.
I don't forget I must have failed to have yours.
If I had a moment.
Just one brief moment to tell you how I feel I'd say,
Hey. I'm so pi**ed. But I love you
    SO much.
I'll forever dream about what might have been.
About the nieces and nephews, maybe I'd have.
About our stories we would have told in the
    storytelling circles our family makes
    on vacations.
I'd tell you that Sublime, Tool, and Smashing
    Pumpkins would still be going strong
    so many years later.
I'd tell you NOTHING has ever been
    the same since you've gone.
I'd say I'm not even sure who I am anymore.

I'd say when those songs come on the

> *radio that mean something to us,*
> *I hope it's not a coincidence.*
> *I hope you know how close I came*
> *to meeting you.*

> *I love you for always.*
> *I miss you forever,*
> *Kori*

When I read this open letter from my best friend to her brother, I cried so hard, knowing how incredibly difficult those words were for her to say. This is what honesty looks like. If we want to get closer to forgiving those who hurt us, we need to be honest about how hanging on to the pain is hurting us. I love the way Kori's letter shows so clearly how taking on the guilt of another's actions makes it impossible to heal. I love that my friend has opened up like this, because sharing how she feels brings her one step closer to keeping the peace of forgiveness.

If you're overwhelmed by guilt, shame, or anger over something you've experienced, maybe it's because the person you actually need to forgive is *you*. In her letter, Kori described how she wanted to feel as low as her brother must have felt out of guilt, so she punished herself. If this line of thinking resonates with you, I want you to know the damage can be undone. The hurt and sadness you feel may stay and are okay, but they don't have to replace your peace. When you release your pain to God, you're not saying it doesn't matter. You're not letting go because you don't care. You're giving yourself permission to learn, grow, and let go so that your mended heart can show love to yourself and others. There's no shortage of laughter when Kori and I are together. We both have experienced deep and traumatic loss. Girltime full of talking it out, swapping memories, and sharing plenty of gut-busting laughs helps us to breathe as we move forward in keeping our peace.

I want you to really think about the thing you've struggled to let go. I know you have it. It has been lumped up in your throat throughout this chapter. Let it out. Cry. Talk to someone. Trust that God will hand out the judgment that is right in His timing, and move forward in your life. To have the humility to forgive those who don't deserve it is such an incredible show of good character in Christ. Being Christlike means loving those who hurt us, loving ourselves enough to move forward, and trusting God to make all things right. Decide for yourself right now to leave it in the past so you can laugh without fear of what your future holds.

She laughs without fear of the future because through forgiveness, she is at peace with her past.

Chapter 9

888

She's a Mess

"No one is righteous—not even one."
ROMANS 3:10

No day created tension between me and my mother like shots day at the doctor's office. When I was little, she had to wrap her legs and arms around my legs and arms like a human straitjacket to keep me from jumping out of the nearest window at the sight of a shot. I built up such a phobia of needles that I didn't care who I had to kick in the shins to get as far away from that syringe as possible. Luckily, Dr. Camp had a wonderful sense of humor, and we'd all laugh about my ridiculousness. I knew I was being irrational. I'd try my best to control my fear in the waiting room by taking deep breaths, bribing my mom, faking a sudden stomach bug, passing out with an Oscar-worthy flop to the floor, and making a last-ditch effort to just go limp on the way to the back. The nurses would cackle and say, "She is a mess."

Even when I was in high school, I remember sitting in the waiting room with my little brother and trying so hard not to freak out knowing what was coming.

He and my mom both sat there cracking up at me and my grown self on the verge of a hissy fit over a shot. I laughed and whined, "Y'all, stop—I can't help it if I don't wanna go get stabbed. Mama, you might have to come back with me when they call my name so you can sit on top of me." A sense of humor about it was the only thing that somewhat calmed my nerves. This fear of needles wasn't really about the needle; it was a fear of pain. Of someone hurting me and me letting them. This fear had me in knots. Is there something you fear that has you "actin' a mess," as my mama always says? Maybe it has you putting off something you know you need to do, like going to the dentist.

I allowed fear to keep me from the dentist for way too long, until I had to face it head-on in the worst way imaginable. I had two wisdom teeth that *had* to come out. My mom didn't have insurance, so anesthesia wasn't an option. I didn't know this until I made my way to the back and got in way too deep to turn around and run. I was in junior college at the time, so I was trying so hard to be brave. They kept assuring me it wouldn't be that bad, and I would be just fine because they would numb my gums. Oh okay, so you're gonna rub some numbing cream on 'em? Nope. I was lying back in the chair trying not to panic when the dental assistant held up the longest, sharpest, most terrifying needle I've ever seen. Y'all, I about died. This was a whole 'nother level—this was not okay. But at this point, all I could do was shift my focus to the assistant talking me through it, and turns out the shot didn't even hurt. But what followed was absolutely terrible. For an hour I had to hear and feel the pressure of cutting, pulling, and twisting going on in my mouth while watching the movie *Purple Rain* on the wall above me. It was torture. Not only the digging around in my mouth, but being forced to watch the artist formerly known as Prince mistreat Apollonia. That was almost more than I could take. I stared at the ceiling while tears rolled down my face, thinking surely they were going to break my jaw, but if they did, at least I'd pass out and be saved from watching this movie. I felt so helpless.

After my wide-awake surgery by Dr. Death, I was fine, but I had a full-blown come-apart when we got in the car. My mama drove me home with a slightly amused, slightly annoyed grin on her face at my over-the-top extra-dramatic requests for unlimited amounts of mashed potatoes from KFC if she wanted to make it up to me. She pulled into the drive-through, exclaiming through a chuckle, "You are such a mess!"

What is it you fear? Maybe it's a broken heart, so you subconsciously push people away by separating yourself. Or perhaps it's rejection, so you keep yourself secluded when invited out or an opportunity arises. Many people are so afraid of maintaining success they don't even try to set the standard. Some are so scared they aren't enough that they never feel the peace of contentment. What does fear look like for you, and how is it impacting your life? How is fear keeping you from just letting loose and causing you to act a mess? Running from your fears is pointless because fear never gets tired, and your shin splints will only take you so far. But when you choose faith and face your fears head-on, your body won't get tired because you won't be running anymore; you'll be flying.

If I was singing a song to Jesus at karaoke, can you guess what it would be? I'll wait. . .you know it. . .sing it with me: *You are the wind beneath my wings. FLYYYY.* . .ack, no, I can't hit that note. Did you? Yeah right, maybe in your head you did. You're such a mess.

I got to witness my mother-in-law make a mad dash when we walked into her worst fear one night. Cats. It was Halloween, and we were out in our neighborhood trick-or-treating. We turned to walk down the next road when we saw a black cat walking toward us. I turned around to warn her, but all I could see was the back of her head running down the middle of the street. I about fell over I was laughing so hard. She couldn't be further from a silly woman, but her phobia of cats had her actin' a straight mess.

Have you ever been to a spooky haunted house? I used to go every fall with friends back before I had kids, when I had better control of my bladder. But the more scared I felt, the harder I laughed uncontrollably. One time, even though I was young, the chain saw chased me so much, I laughed tears straight down my leg into my shoe.

I recently took my kids to the carnival, and against my better judgment, I decided to get on a ride called the Hurricane with my two older daughters. I regret that decision. I quickly remembered the age of my ticker the first time we dropped down going ninety hundred miles an hour while spinning in circles. Little did I know my oldest was recording us, and between screeches and screams, we were all laughing hysterically. I didn't feel right the whole rest of the day. I guess those warning signs outside the ride that say *Hey, old fart, don't put yourself in dangerous situations if your heart can't take it* now apply to me. But sometimes when we are face-to-face with fear, our body's physical response is laughter. It calms us down before we give ourselves a heart attack. A good nervous giggle helps the adrenaline settle before you act a mess and—worst-case scenario—mess your pants.

Yes, I'm a mess. So are you, and so is everyone you know. Apparently, it's genetic. I got a taste of my own medicine when I took my own child to the doctor and she ended up having strep throat. Options were to get the steroid shot and feel better in a day or take antibiotics at the same time every day for two weeks. I'm not so great at making sure meds get taken the same time every day. Just ask my OB/GYN. So we went with the shot. She did good until the nurse came in, set the syringe on the counter, and let us know she'd have to roll over and take the shot in her butt cheek. All of a sudden, my sweet, obedient, type A nine-year-old who does everything she's told turned into an immovable stubborn mule. Not because of the shot so much as the mention of the word *butt*. She was panicking, and I couldn't make her understand she wasn't gonna have to moon the nurse, just pull the top of her shorts down a bit. Not even far enough to see her crack. I showed her on myself where it would be, thinking that would help, but I'll be derned if I didn't make it worse when my big, long crack peeked out like it always does. I tried to explain to her that mom cracks are just longer, but she was refusing to flip over. Now, as her mother, I understood that she wasn't just being difficult or disobedient; she is just really modest and private. So I'm trying to do the whole mom-therapist thing and talk her down. But the nurse didn't have time to play games, so in the middle of my breathing exercise, she basically picked her up and flipped her over. I wasn't sure if I should be aggravated or thankful that the nurse just manhandled my daughter, but therapy wasn't working, and we didn't have all day. The shot took two seconds, nobody saw her butt, and she learned a valuable lesson about having to do things we don't want to sometimes. Because life is like that nurse, and it will manhandle you if you don't do what you need to do. We got in the car and I was joking with her that she took it sort of, kind of, a little bit like a champ. She tried not to giggle because she wanted to be mad, so I told her about my mama having to hold me down for shots too. I told her there are so many things more painful than getting a shot, and I kid you not, this was her response: "Like what? Death?" I looked at her and she looked at me, and then we both laughed so hard we couldn't breathe. I thought to myself, *She is such a mess.*

Being called "a mess" in my family was a good thing. Usually you were called that while cracking everyone up. It's a good character trait to have. Especially in moments of frustration that would make most people mad. Like that one time the devil tried to steal my joy when I stepped on a melted piece of gum. I was walking through a parking lot heading back to my car when a brake light popped on and a car started rolling in reverse while I was just on the verge of passing behind it. I had to skedaddle my happy butt out of the way. The driver must've had no depth perception because they honked their horn at *me* when I was clearly within the pedestrian passing zone right behind their back tire. *Swing and a miss, Devil—I will not be a bumper sticker today*, I thought to myself. About two steps later, I felt it. The dreaded tug on the sole of my flip-flop that we all know the minute we feel it. Melted gum. I looked down and I'm telling y'all, I've never seen anything like it. This was the sticky spearmint of Satan himself. It had stretched and wrapped around the back of my flip-flop like it was trying to grab my ankle to keep me from dodging another car. I got so mad, I actually found myself looking around for the chewer so I could wave my flip-flop around in their face and make scary noises. I got in my car convinced the enemy had just launched a spiritual attack against me through my chewing gum shoe.

When you're trying to walk with the Lord, you can guarantee the enemy will put some melted Bubble Yum in your path. Don't you let him get you stuck. That's why I always carry the wet wipes of Christ in my car. One swipe will set you free. There ain't no gum so sticky that the wipes of Christ can't clean it right off! Amen, sister—there are miracles everywhere; you just gotta see 'em. That's not all those wipes can do either. When the enemy tempts you to wipe your booger under the front seat, you got the wet wipes of Christ keeping it clean. 'Cause that's unsanitary just like Satan is. When you forgot deodorant and your body odor's so bad it's downright evil, that smell from hell don't stand a chance when you got the wipes to cleanse you of all your stench. Whew, it might not be a Sunday, but I'm gonna take ya to church. Not today, Devil! You can't steal my joy when I belong to Jesus. He blessed this mess with a way to see humor in all things, including the ways I can work the silliest stresses into my faith. As I sat laughing in my car, I realized I've learned some of the most important life lessons from everyday annoyances.

Having a sense of humor in life is like having the wet wipes of Christ with you everywhere you go in case something frustrating or embarrassing pops up. Whether it's gum on your shoe, a lady banging her car door into your car and then giving *you* a dirty look, two cars in a row going from the same spot at a four-way-stop (help me, Lord), or your toddler running their tongue down the front counter at Chick-fil-A, your humor is God's way of helping you laugh it off so you don't flip out. When life starts to feel overwhelmed with stress, use the gift of humor to just "be a mess."

I never met a woman trying to be perfect who could let loose, enjoy things, let things go, and laugh. Walking on eggshells isn't good for your feet, so kick them up and relax a little. It's the little things driving you nuts that could be cracking you up. Have you ever read *The Life-Changing Magic of Company's Coming*? Well, that's because I haven't written it yet. It's gonna be a how-to book about making your home appear as if you actually do chores on the daily in twenty minutes or less when you get word company's coming over. All you gotta do is toss every extra item on your tables and floors in a bedroom and lock the door. And I mean *everything*. The random never-used toddler swim shoe that your puppy likes to chew, all the papers that are just every-where (including artwork, flyers, wrappers, bills, and *unopened* Publishers Clearing House envelopes that I won't be falling for again), ride-on toys, clean laundry piled in a basket, all of it. Then you make sure every-one in the house knows not to ever, under any circum-stance, open a bedroom door. Next you put all the dirty dishes in the oven and repeat to yourself, *Don't burn the dishes, don't burn the dishes*, so you won't forget and burn the dishes. Pick up the dirty towels and underwear off the bathroom floor, sling 'em in the tub, and pull the curtain shut. Last but not least, light a candle. My favorite scent is *deception*. When they leave, you can relax, preheat the oven for some yummy frozen pizza, and wait for the smell of burning Tupperware to re-mind you about the dishes. Putting on a show of perfect sounds like a peaceful way to live life, doesn't it?

Can you think of a recent example in your own life when you were too uptight to enjoy things? Maybe you hosted a party and couldn't even have fun. Or worried too much about your Cheeto-stained thumb to enjoy a hand massage. How about a pool day wasted away on comparing imperfections instead of slipping and splashing? I hope when I'm doing cannonballs, having chicken fights, doing flips, and laughing hysterically with my kids, people do look and say, "She's a mess." She's a mess, and she's happy because she is free from worry of what others think.

When my kids get out of the car in the school drop-off line, sometimes their backpacks accidentally drag all the car's floorboard trash with them. We have a car that's lived in, okay? You might find a sock, a ziplock baggie of dried-up carrots, all the papers sent home from school the week before, and CVS receipts that could reach all the way from the car to the school entrance. One morning they opened the door with me yelling, "Don't drag the trash!" right before they dragged all the trash and took off running like they didn't hear me. I had to throw the car in park and sprint braless, wearing flip-flops and pajama bottoms, around the parking lot to pick up all the papers blowing in the wind, because I may be a mess, but I don't litter—all while laughing hysterically and yelling, "Don't look at me!" to the mom behind us in line whose lipstick was the exact shade as her Lululemon jacket. That was a scary moment. It was either litter or completely embarrass myself with faith that God could work even this out for good. So I chose faith, and if you laughed at that story, then it worked. Laughing people are happy, and happy people don't hurt people. You're welcome.

There are a couple of things I don't find funny. Boogers and farts. Nothing gets under my skin like someone picking their nose without a tissue and flicking it or wiping it Lord knows where. I need a wet wipe of Christ to scrub off the irritation about to set me off when I see all the boogers my child has wiped on her nightstand. One time my best friend brought her baby over for a playdate and we were in my little one's bedroom while she changed her baby's diaper. She dug a boogie from her child's nose, and as I reached for a wipe to give her, I watched with eyes wide in panic as she wiped it *on my carpet.* I looked at her and said, "Okay, you'd better find that booger right now and put it in this wipe and throw it out, because if you don't, I will be up all night with a magnifying glass searching out this boogie that doesn't even genetically belong to one of mine." She laughed so hard because there are very few things that truly bother me. She's a mess too, so just picking her kid's booger and wiping it had become muscle memory at that point. She didn't even realize she'd done it until I started waving a wipe around and freaking out. Y'all might find that funny, but that's a mess I can't get behind. That, and being forced to breathe someone else's butt air. That is what it is. And I don't want it in my mouth or up my nose. I don't so much as giggle when my husband runs me out of the room. You have stolen my ability to breathe in my own living room, and I am offended.

I know not everyone is able to find the funny in everyday life. You don't have to be silly, goofy, or a full-blown mess in order to find the bright side. I've had plenty of seasons when nothing was funny and I could hardly smile. Here are a few things you can do when the struggle is serious and the mess you find yourself in just isn't funny.

- *Go to a comedy show. Even if you don't find the comic that funny, being in an environment where laughter is welcome and present will ease your tension and lighten your spirit. Hearing laughter helps you feel connected to others.*

- *Watch a funny movie or a lighthearted TV show, or scroll through the funniest compilations of YouTube videos you can find. Surely you can find something that'll bump your tickle bone. One of our favorite Sunday traditions as a family has always been watching* America's Funniest Home Videos. *It doesn't matter how rough the week has been or how stressful the week ahead is gonna be, I feel nothing but gratitude and joy sitting with my family and hearing the sweet sounds of them laughing.*

- *If you have a friend or family member who is mess enough for both of you, call them up and go out to lunch. When one of you is silly and one of you is a little more uptight, you rub off on each other. Those kinds of connections create a pretty great balance between loosening up and taking things more seriously.*

Comedy, goofy things, and carefree personalities exist for a reason. We all have gifts, and if being a little nutty just isn't one of yours, that's okay—you can sit back and enjoy the hilarious mess of others.

She's a mess, and she is loved exactly as she is. Flaws

and all. She's the kind of mess you don't wanna clean up. She's goofy and she's fun, and sometimes she comes undone. She's perfectly imperfect. She laughs because she deserves it. Life is too short to spend it all wound up. Use the humor God has gifted you with to pick your battles. You have a spirit that longs for joy, and there's no joy in always trying to keep it together. *She laughs* because the humor in things is easy to see when life gets messy.

Chapter 10

She Laughs

"For I know the plans I have for you," declares the LORD, "plans to prosper you and not to harm you, plans to give you hope and a future."

JEREMIAH 29:11 NIV

When we sat on the floor of our single-wide trailer—a home that offered little more than shelter—we laughed. We laughed hard and often, and most important, we laughed together. Our humor kept us focused on what mattered when we had nothing much materially.

When an old boyfriend spent two years emotionally abusing me, playing games with me, breaking up with me and then begging me back, my friends got me through it with food, dancing, movies, and their sweet company as we talked and laughed until we ran out of breath.

When my child makes things awkward in the public bathroom by groaning loudly like she's giving birth before announcing to everybody that her big poopin' is out of her butt, the other mothers let me know they get it when we make eye contact and laugh.

When I looked at my crush cracking up one night

while we all sat on his porch, I knew my feelings for him were real because as I told my funny story in all my vulnerable goofy glory, he laughed. He laughed at me, I kissed him, and now we have three children.

When my niece slipped into depression as she fought cancer in isolation, it was only laughter that lifted her up. And when we buried her fifteen months later, it was only laughter after the funeral over a game of Aggravation that allowed us to cope until the next day.

The ability to laugh is the gift we've been given to conquer fearful feelings. It is the glowing green stars on the bedroom ceiling that we look at when monsters make it hard to sleep. It shifts our focus and makes us okay long enough to get through the hardest days. It is a physical manifestation of the joy our spirits carry. A woman who laughs is a woman who perseveres, who isn't afraid to be gritty in the pursuit of purpose and peace.

Speaking of grit, I wrote you a poem. I was thinking one day how unlikely it seems that someone like me would eventually write about her faith. Even still I battle the residue of opinions that people have left in my thoughts. But the Holy Spirit dwelling within me reminded me that grace for the gritty is never pretty. So for all my girls with grit, I went with it. . . .

GRIT AND GRACE

My journey to Jesus has been more
*   gritty than pretty.*
But I'm a girl after God despite how you see me.
I know it seems odd.
Someone like me could be used by God?
But just the same,
He's calling my name.
So I'll listen when He teaches.
Usually in my struggling seasons.
In all these fleshly messes,
I'm learning lots of lessons.
Based on my past you'd call me trashy.
But He gives me beauty when I'm ashy.
When people judge don't you listen.
There's too much purpose you'd be missin'.
God has called you with all your flaws.
'Cause people like you can reach the lost.
It's the toughest of your stuff that makes
*   you Oddly Enough.*
She laughs without fear of the future.
There's always hope as long as there's humor.

So smile through mistakes 'cause there
will be plenty.
Grace for the gritty never looks pretty.

I think deep down we usually know what we need to do. The back-and-forth, overthinking, and stress are the fear. The woman who is dignified, empowered, and unshaken by fear is described as laughing. Laughter is the antithesis of fear. It lightens the mood and the air in the room. Without laughter, I don't think I would be here. It is truly a gift.

Maybe you've been in a season lately where you've lost your laughter. Maybe you've been feeling afraid of disappointment, rejection, failure, or loss. I want you to know it's okay. Sometimes feeling afraid is what makes you feel like a failure in your faith. But it isn't that she laughs without fear altogether; it's that she isn't afraid of the future. Why? At the end of the day, no matter what she's feeling, she knows that God is good. Bottom line. That one fact never changes.

I have spent the better part of the past year wrapped up in uncontrollable anxiety. I have felt worried and unworthy time and time again. I've been crushed under the weight of a fear of disappointing others. I've felt like a failure as a wife, a mother, and a friend. I've doubted myself as an author. All of it stemmed from expectations of people and the fear that I can't give them what they need from me. You know what was missing in the midst of all this stressing? Roots in the truth.

You will experience times in life when the world chips away at you until you break loose. God has called you out onto the water, but the enemy doesn't want to see you walk across. So he uses strongholds of your past, other people, popular voices and opinions, and even family and friends to stir up enough fear that you sink and forget you can swim.

The enemy uses fear to make you feel like you're drowning, but here's why she laughs. She serves a God who will part the water so she can walk out instead of staying under. All you have to do is move your feet. There's no such thing as failing when you serve a God whose *love* never fails. Whether you walk on water or sink to the bottom, He is there. He never leaves you, forsakes you, shames you, or blames you. Why hasn't the enemy learned by now that there's nothing you can throw at a woman of God that can keep her down? She laughs when you try, because with every struggling season her testimony only deepens.

Every fear that yanks me up from my roots only makes them that much stronger when I remember the power of my Father. We will always reconnect. You have nothing to fear, but when you feel afraid anyway, don't let anxiety swallow you whole. We serve a God who is with us through it all. Fear doesn't keep us from moving because we walk by faith not by sight (2 Corinthians 5:7). When the path isn't clear, when our connection is foggy, we don't fear because we know He hasn't gone anywhere. I can always come out of the darkest of places knowing when the hard times pass, I will just give Him more praises. Being incapable of feeling happy is torture, but experiencing joy once again is exhilarating. If you never had to carry heavy struggles, you'd never know the sweet relief when the weight is replaced with His peace.

Let's be honest, finishing this book will bring the greatest peace I've felt in a while. But the anxiety wrapped up in publishing good words is worth every bit of fulfilling my calling. We need to push forward through fears for no other reason than we *can*. We can get to the other side of it if we keep walking. Don't worry about what you will have to experience in order to learn; instead, focus on why God is teaching you the lesson. Since His plans for you are good, there's no telling what will come from whatever wilderness you're currently wandering.

I used to really stress out about how far I feel sometimes from the woman of God I want to be. This Proverbs woman who is clothed in strength—she isn't the picture of perfection you may imagine. Her flesh needs to be covered in the power of Christ because it is weak. She isn't free of failure; she is prepared for it. She knows better than to think she won't make a mistake. She gets scared, but she doesn't stay there. She strives to let go, but sometimes she doesn't. Grief takes time, after all. She yearns to be better, and she knows who Christ says she is. She fights the urges of her flesh and the enticements of the world so she can come back to a faith so fresh it's like that of a little girl. She breaks now and then, exhausted from the war playing out between her mind and her spirit, but she has dignity derived from grace. Nothing can be taken from her that the spirit of Christ won't replace.

She is human. She is you; she is me; she is goals. And the purpose of having a goal isn't just to achieve it—it's to mold you into the person you'd have to be to get anywhere near it. As you grow to be a woman who can laugh without fear, you'll have to continue to learn. Because you're not her yet. Nobody is. There will always be something we need to improve on. That's what life is: steps forward in growth until you get distracted and walk your face into a flagpole. With so many steps forward and back, thank goodness for the ability to laugh. That's why we don't have to fear anything in the future. Nothing is coming at us that God can't use *for* us if we let Him. She lets Him. She waits patiently, and when God calls her off the bench to learn a lesson, she chooses to play. If pride starts to get in the way, she knows she'll be humbled. She cares; her heart hopes to make someone's life better. She speaks when the time is right, and she holds her tongue when she wants to fight. Sometimes she fights. When she does, she learns who she doesn't want to be—unless the fight is for something that gives God glory. She puts herself in a position to listen when she's missing a connection. Whether she gets alone in the car in the garage or just spends a moment praying in the parking lot before heading into the store to buy groceries. She takes the opportunity to just be. To be free from the chatter so she can hear the One who matters.

This might sound weird, but I used to fear the

idea of heaven. Most people find comfort in knowing death isn't the end. But when I'd sit and really imagine eternity, it would fill me with anxiety. Something about the idea of never-ending forever made me panic. There was something comforting to me about the notion of an end, a final chapter that closes the book and lets me just be done. For some reason, something about death felt kind of like relief. And the thought of forever with no clear structure gave me a feeling of fear. It still kind of does. I think what really scares me though, is any kind of unknown change. I can't wait to be in the presence of my Savior and feel perfect peace at last. But I have a healthy fear of God as I should, and I'm not looking forward to having all my sins laid bare. Thankfully, a day is like an hour, so I hear, so maybe it'll only take a year. When anxiety creeps into my chest at thoughts of the unknown, I try to remember this world has never been my home. What I do know is that in heaven there is no fear. No anxiety, depression, or unrest. I'll feel like I never left. It's my flesh that freaks out, but in my spirit there's no doubt that eternity is my deepest longing. The end of all the pain that comes with sin and the beginning of perfect joy in Jesus' presence.

Fear isn't going anywhere. But whether it controls

you is up to you. Personally, my greatest fear is disappointing people. I could be called every name in the book, but when someone says, "I'm disappointed in you," my heart begins to throb. It feels like such a personal attack on *who* I am as if I'm not allowed to displease anyone *ever*, which is impossible. I can get worked up feeling like the things I do and the parts of me I can't change are not enough. Sometimes this feeling of inadequacy makes me want to give up. I'd like to say that I'm no quitter, but under enough stress, I've had a tendency to just walk away. To toss out every ounce of belief I had in myself and accept that what others think of me is true. If people are never going to be pleased with me, I'll just cut them off. The best way to avoid hearing that I've disappointed someone is to just stay quiet and keep everyone at a distance. I can shut myself off from others and limit expectations by keeping everyone far enough away that they'd never even know the calling I felt on my life. It's a calling that requires a public display of my thoughts, mistakes, experiences, and faith. Scrutiny will not be escaped. It's no coincidence that my calling aligns perfectly with my greatest fear.

What keeps me from walking away? Let's recap. I said in the beginning that I wanted to know who this woman is. What it is she has that helps her keep fear from dictating her future, that prevents her from standing still or walking away. What I've learned before and after living with Christ in my heart is that we can't move forward with fear on our own. The Holy Spirit gives us gifts that enable us to move forward despite our fears. So I based all the topics we covered on the character of a woman who laughs because she is at peace with what her future holds.

Your ability to laugh is precious. Fight for it. Protect it. In a world that wants to drain your joy, your laugh gives hope a voice. Speak that life into your spirit. Keep your faith. Make mistakes. Learn from failures. Stay humbled. Break down when you need to. Listen to the voice of truth. Never quit playing. Fail as often as it takes for your calling to take shape. Feel fear all you want, but always choose faith. Be imperfect in public. And for goodness' sake. . .do not *ever* clip your toenails in someone's bed. Keep it light, friends.

When I was going through hard times this past year, I wrote a prayer of thanks for the reminder that it's okay. That's what faith and laughter are for.

> *"Hi, God. It's been awhile. Since I've prayed.*
> *Since I've smiled. I mean, I've smiled I suppose,*
> *but it wasn't true, heaven knows. You've seen*

me struggling against the strongholds, the lies, and the fears this year. I know better, and here come the tears. I guess I'm not supposed to have it all figured out. You keep me tripping on my guessing. You're humorous like that. Some say it's rude to laugh when someone falls, but without a sense of humor, I might not get back up at all. Dignity can be found on the ground, and strength is restored on the floor. That's where my knees are meant to be. Thank You for reminding me. Thank You for the gift of laughter. I cherish it always. I know as long as I can laugh, I keep the joy of hope for my future. In Jesus' holy and precious name, amen.

We laugh because we can. Simple as that.

If you enjoyed *She Laughs*,
check out Carolanne Miljavac's
Odd(ly) Enough!

Turn the page to read more.

INTRODUCTION

*"My grace is sufficient for you,
for my power is made perfect in weakness."*
2 Corinthians 12:9 NIV

Isn't it odd how God works? All the mysterious ways His plans come together with who He crafted us to be.

Have you ever taken the time to look back on all the moments you didn't think you'd survive, and recognized the purpose in your pain? Or maybe you've been stuck in the mud, unable to see any value in your struggle. Sometimes we get so bogged down by self-doubt that we can't see any potential for a better life. But know this: the greatest lie the enemy has ever whispered into your thoughts is that you aren't *enough*.

Have you ever had thoughts like this scamper through your mind?

You're not. . .

Good enough.

Smart enough.

Pretty enough.

Rich enough.

Kind enough.

Talented enough.

Loved enough.

Enough already, Satan! We get it! The evil one, the fallen angel determined to destroy those carrying the Spirit of Christ, is on a mission to convince us of all the things we know to be true about *him*. He hates the potential and redemption of those more powerful than he'll ever be. The misfits. The oddballs. The unqualified. The ones called to defy the standards of the world and stand in his way.

Yes, we are easy targets. We emerge from ditches, broken hearts, and bondage. Minds can be easily manipulated when spirits are broken. This was true for me. I wanted nothing more than to fit in from the time I was a child. By society's standards, I was poor white trash from a trailer park. Destined to become a teen mom and a drug addict, contributing nothing to society and living out my days in poverty. Many times I attempted to prove society right. Believe me when I tell you I tried really hard to throw my life away. Every inkling of purpose that crept up in my heart was immediately shoved down in disbelief. I know you've been there too. I didn't know it then, but God had other plans. What I was blind to back then, I now can see clearly. This is exactly how it needed to be: I needed to make mistakes so I could look back and marvel at the miracle of God's plan for my life.

It took a lot of wandering in the wilderness to

build the character I'd need for His calling. I was weak in my wilderness, and like 2 Corinthians 12:9 says, it is there that *His* power is made perfect. It is in our greatest moments of imperfection, when we are broken and humbled, aware of our need for God, that He comes in and shows us the beauty in our ashes. So everything that we think makes us an outcast is actually what makes us. . .oddly. . .*enough*. If you've ever felt insignificant, out of place, uncomfortable, or unqualified, I want to encourage you that it doesn't matter where you come from, what you've done, or what has been done to you. You have been qualified by the character built in your fall. The hardest parts of your life have given you the greatest value.

By the time you finish this book, I trust you'll believe that with all of your heart. I'm going to be completely bare, vulnerable, and transparent with my own life stories. A little bit of good alongside a whole lot of bad and ugly. Through poverty, molestation, bullying, sex, drugs, depression, and tragedy, God never gave up on me, and He'll never give up on you. So let's get naked. Okay, not legiterally. Keep your clothes on. Just keep reading.

About the Author

Carolanne Miljavac is a southern-raised, Jesus-saved, barely sane author, speaker, social media goofball, wife, and mom of three daughters. It was the crushing loss of her seven-year-old niece to cancer that finally humbled her enough to listen to God when He said to her, as she crumbled in her car, *"Give it up."* Without the chains of fear and insecurity, she followed her spirit's instruction to speak. She now has over 100 million video views and more than half a million social media followers. A true reflection of "beauty for ashes," Carolanne has become the go-to girl for a good laugh, motivation, loving truths, and vulnerability. She pulls heartstrings while tapping funny bones with a message of freedom and revelation. Her purpose in life is to spread love and joy without sacrificing honesty and truth. She believes we all have a story needing to be told. Grief taught her gratitude, pain gave her purpose, and loss revealed true love. With faith, she found audacity, and her mission is to give you the guts to be *you* too.

More Inspiration and Humor from Carolanne Miljavac!

Odd(ly) Enough: 3-Minute Devotions to Passionately Pursuing Your Purpose

You'll discover the message your uncertain, hurting heart needs to hear in *Odd(ly) Enough: 3-Minute Devotions to Passionately Pursuing Your Purpose*. 180 uplifting devotions from social media star CA Miljavac pack a powerful dose of comfort, encouragement, and inspiration into just-right-sized readings, perfect for your busy schedule.

- Minute 1: meditate on a brief scripture selection
- Minute 2: read a short devotional
- Minute 3: say a prayer and begin a conversation with God. Each day's reading will meet you right where you are and is the ideal way for you to begin or end your day.

Paperback / 978-1-64352-324-8 / $9.99

Odd(ly) Enough

Humorous. Authentic. Relatable. That's Carolanne Miljavac in a nutshell. And those qualities are just what her nearly half a million social media followers adore about her. Her *Odd(ly) Enough* is a message that your heart needs to hear: *It's time to embrace the "you" God made you to be. Tune out the naysayers of the world and jump into His loving arms. He'll walk alongside you as you passionately pursue your God-given purpose.* With chapters like "Who Do You Think You Are?," "Control Freak," and "Mistakes and Grace," you will find yourself becoming a little more courageous. . .and a *lot more* confident about God's purpose for your life.

Paperback / 978-1-68322-789-2 / $14.99